The G-K PROJECT

THE G-K PROJECT
A Peace Corps Experience

A Peace Corps Writers Book - an imprint of Peace Corps Worldwide

Printed in the United States of America
By Peace Corps Writers of Oakland, California.

For more information, contact peacecorpsworldwide@gmail.com.

Peace Corps Writers and the Peace Corps Writers colophon
are trademarks of PeaceCorpsWorldwide.org.

Book design and cover creation by Dania Zafar.

ISBN-13:978-1-950444-24-3
Library of Congress Control Number: 2021901209

First Peace Corps Writers Edition, January 2021

The G-K PROJECT

A Peace Corps Experience

CARL MURRY

A PEACE CORPS WRITERS BOOK

Contents

This book is dedicated to my grandson
Beauregard Price Bachtelle

PREFACE

One-Town World

Imagine that we could compress this world population of more than 2 ½ billion into one town of 1,000 persons in the exact proportions in which the world population is actually divided. In such a town of 1,000 there would be only 60 Americans! And these 60 Americans would receive half the income of the entire town. Only about 330 of the remaining 940 townspeople would be classified as Christians. At least 80 townspeople would be practicing Communists and 370 others under Communist domination

The 60 Americans would have an average life expectancy of 70 years; the other 940 less than 40 years. The Americans would have 15 times as many possessions per person as all of their Neighbors. The Americans would produce 16 percent of the town's food supply and although they would eat 72 percent above the maximum food requirements, they would eat most of what they grew, or store it for their further use, at enormous cost. (With most of the 940 non Americans hungry, the food disparity might understandably lead to some ill feeling.) There would be 53 telephones in this one - town world .... Americans would have 28 of them. The Americans would also enjoy a disportionate share of the electric power, coal, fuel, steel, and general equipment.

The lowest income group among the Americans would be better off by far than the average of the other townsmen. The 60 Americans and about 200 others representing Western Europe and a few classes in South America, South Africa, Australia and Japan would be relatively well off, by comparison.

Half of the inhabitants of our one-town world would be ignorant of Jesus Christ, but more than half of them would have heard, and would continue to hear, of Karl Marx, Lenin, Stalin, and Khrushchev.

Could this one-town world survive? If you were one of the 60 American townsfolk, what would you do to preserve this tiny world? Chances are you would be plenty worried about the problem. Chances are that you would do something. What do you think it would be?

FROM: "PG&E PROGRESS", AUGUST 1961

My "Philosophy of Education" class assigned us to read and discuss this article published by PG&E titled "A One Town World." The role of education was a focal point and had a significant impact on my political identity and life goals. These are some of the opinions in the class. How would you respond?

"There seem to be two main approaches to the problem, either isolation or inclusion. We build walls, or we build bridges."

"Building walls provides a sense of security for the short term, but if the ninety percent are desperate, they would lay siege or destroy them."

"Our technical and military expertise is superior and could be used to keep them under control."

"There would not be enough resources for all to share equally."

"The development and allocation of the world's resources could be entrusted to representatives of the state for equal distribution."

"Maybe the various cultures do not value material goods as much as we do and would be satisfied with basic human needs."

"We need all the resources we can get to sustain our growth, so interaction with the rest of the world is necessary."

"It is our best interest to assist the other countries of the world with education, agriculture, health, and their basic human needs."

CHOICES

CHAPTER 1

How It Started

My first presidential election was coming up as I entered my senior year in the fall of 1960 at Cal-Poly in San Luis Obispo. My twenty-first birthday was on June 5, and Carol and I married a week later, on June 12.

"My folks are voting for Nixon, but I don't know if I will."

"Why do they like him?" asked Carol.

"Well, he has the experience of being Vice President, he is from California, and they can trust him more than Kennedy," I answered.

"Trust him?"

"You know, Kennedy is just a young rich kid from a political family back East, and he is Catholic and might take orders from the Pope."

"Seriously, do you believe that?" she replied.

"Well, I don't know, but I really like Kennedy's energy, enthusiasm, and ideas. He feels like a leader I could follow."

"Did you hear that Ted Kennedy will be coming to Cal-Poly in early October?"

"Yeah, let's make sure we can go to hear him."

Two weeks later, we stood on the lawn in front of the library as Ted Kennedy arrived with enthusiasm and a big smile. His presentation was short and went to questions and answers quickly. During his concluding remarks, he asked any of us interested in the volunteer program for overseas service to meet with him in the basement conference room in the library. He explained the concept as originally proposed by Senators Reuss and Humphrey and developed by candidate John Kennedy. He asked for input on feasibility, ideas for application, selection, safety, preparation, types of jobs, etc.

"What do you think?" asked Carol.

"Wow! Lots of mixed feelings from being excited to scared. There are so many things to consider. Do you think it has a chance of happening?"

"I don't know, but I am excited about doing something really meaningful like that."

"Yeah, me too, and I have decided that I am going to vote for John Kennedy in a couple of weeks. Hey, are we still planning to go to Troutner's next Saturday to listen to the Cal-Poly football game against Bowling Green?"

"Sure, they are planning a Halloween theme party after the game, and it sounds like fun," she said with a big grin.

"As long as it doesn't interfere with the game. It would have been a lot of fun to travel with the guys to Ohio. Last year, our longest trip was to Montana."

"Yeah, yeah, you never got to play much anyway. Let's stop by the farm and get some salad stuff on our way home, OK?"

Our home was a thirty-foot Mayflower trailer parked on a ranch in Los Osos Valley where we did chores, milked the cow, and tutored the landlord's kids to work off our twenty dollar a month rent. Dr. Dan and Judy Chase had three children and were like family to us.

CHAPTER 2

Some Background

Carol and I decided to marry at the beginning of my senior year, and we attend Cal-Poly for one year until I completed my B.S. degree. We would then move to Santa Barbara, and I would work until she completed her degree and then move back to Cal-Poly to finish my 5th year for a teaching credential while she worked.

We both attended Hughson High School and began dating in the spring of my senior year. After high school, I planned to join the Navy with two of my best friends, but we ended up going to Modesto Junior College, where I played football, took agriculture classes, and continued dating Carol.

After Carol graduated high school, we both attended MJC. for one year. She was bright and had a choice of Universities to attend and chose UC Santa Barbara. We were pretty young to get married and decided to go to our separate schools for a year and see how it went.

The college environment provided opportunities to learn about other cultures through interactions with foreign students. We both made several friendships that sparked an interest in them and their countries. Hamid, from Lebanon, was a fellow Crops major and invited me to visit his father's citrus orchards.

Making the football team helped me financially by providing my tuition, room and board, and kept me busy during the fall semester. One of my part-time jobs was working at a Shell Service station on the weekends. In March of 1960, just before spring training was to begin, a car rolled off the lube rack and pinned me between it and a parked car. The accident crushed my left ankle between the bumpers, and my football days were over.

Bill Troutner was Department Head for Crops and a classmate and friend of Carol's dad when they attended the University of California at Davis together and took us under his wing now and then. We showed up early at their home to listen to the game on the radio because of the Eastern Time zone, and we were enjoying the Halloween party when a news alert informed us that the team plane had crashed during takeoff, and twenty-two of my teammates had died.

As it turned out, the injury to my ankle not only kept me from being on that plane but would have a huge impact on the direction my life would take.

CHAPTER 3

Making Application

John F. Kennedy won the November 8 election by a narrow margin. In his inaugural address on January 20, 1961, he stated, "Ask not what your country can do for you but what you can do for your country." He then announced his intent to establish the Peace Corps.

"So it is really going to happen; do we want to do it now or not?"

"Well, it would be better to finish college first and kinda see how it works before we jump into it. I wonder about the danger and health risks, and since we would be volunteering, could we afford it?" I offered.

"Married couples cannot serve if they have children. You could be drafted and may not physically qualify with the ankle injury. It could be risky to wait. Besides, I am excited to help get this started and for it to succeed!"

"Yeah, me too. There are so many things that have to come together for it to work, and I would really regret missing the opportunity."

On March 1, 1961, President Kennedy officially created the Peace Corps by executive order and appointed Sargent

Shriver Jr. as its director. We submitted our application forms and asked to report to the Post Office in San Luis Obispo on the second Saturday in April to take a battery of tests, including General Aptitude, Language Aptitude, and our Technical fields. Two weeks later, the Peace Corps informed us that our test results were very good, and our skills were in high demand.

We were on our way.

CHAPTER 4

Selection Process

A letter from Thomas Quimby that arrived on June 19, 1961, informed us that Peace Corps had selected us for projects in Burma and to standby for an invitation to training. With finals finishing up, we scoured the library for maps, photos, and information on Burma and waited for our invitation.

"What should we do now that we have finished our finals?"

"Let's just go ahead with our plan to go home and work until we hear from them. If we continue with school, we will need the money, and we need to take the trailer back to Hughson anyway!"

In early June, we were informed that the USA and Burma were unable to reach an agreement on establishing a program. They transferred our applications to a project in Chile, and training would begin in July at the University of Notre Dame. We continued our summer jobs and started learning about Chile until we received a phone call informing us that it was difficult to find positions for us in the same area, but if we were willing for Carol to live in Santiago and me to live at an agriculture extension site about 100 miles south of Santiago, they had a placement for us. We declined the invitation with regret because we wanted to live together. They could forward our applications to projects in Ghana and Tanzania if we were interested. Of course, we were. We began researching these new countries.

We continued our jobs, and the summer passed quickly. I was driving a truck, operating a forklift, and helping with the family fruit harvest. Carol interned at a medical lab in Modesto. The Peace Corps notified us that they had filled all positions in the African projects, but a program in India was in the works. With a little less enthusiasm, we began to study India and returned to our plan to finish school.

In Goleta, we found a trailer park near UC Santa Barbara, and Carol enrolled in her third semester. I found work as a maintenance man in a housing development called Hidden Valley Homes and did part-time jobs, which included working nights at a drive-in movie and hauling "Fall Out Shelters" down to the Los Angeles area on some weekends.

During the fall, recruitment programs slowed as Peace Corps implemented and refined first projects and modified training. They scaled down the Puerto Rico survival model, and it became a part of the pre-service training. There were projects in Columbia and then Borneo that Peace Corps considered us for, and we researched those countries.

Cal Poly is on a quarter system while UC is on the semester system, so we had an overlap of about six weeks, where we were both in class. I returned to Cal Poly to begin my fifth-year program in early January. Since Carol needed our VW bug to get to school, I was able to stay on a friend's couch and walk to school and around campus in San Luis Obispo. On weekends, I would hitchhike the ninety miles to Goleta, which created many adventurous memories. At the end of February 1962, we moved the trailer to the Silver City Trailer Park, and Carol began working at the local hospital.

During March and April, we did not hear anything from the Peace Corps and began calling in regard to our status. In early May, we received a call from Sargent Shriver's office apologizing and explaining that they had misplaced our applications after the Borneo invitation, and we would hear from them soon.

On May 29, 1962, we received an invitation for the Pakistan project, or, if we preferred, there was an agriculture extension project in Thailand starting around the same date. Since I had listed Agriculture Teacher as my preferred job, we chose Pakistan. Training was to begin July 7 at the University of Minnesota, St. Paul Campus, and we would stay in Bailey Hall. Airline tickets would arrive around June 15.

On May 30, I called my folks to inform them of our assignment and arrange for them to help haul our trailer home after finals, which started on Monday, June 11. The last week of school was a whirlwind of activity, finishing classes, looking up information on Pakistan, finishing my part-time jobs, and making arrangements for the move back to Hughson.

On Friday, June 9, I returned from my last class to find a telegram from my draft board in Modesto informing me that my education deferment had expired. They ordered me to report for induction on Monday, June 11, at 6:30 am. The Berlin Crisis in May of 1962 was probably the reason for the urgent call-up.

It may be helpful to describe the political atmosphere of that time. In the early fifties, we watched the testing of atomic bombs on television and newsreels. We felt the earth shake and watched the mushroom clouds bloom over the Sierra Nevada Mountains from the test sites in Nevada.

The race with Russia was on to see who could develop the biggest and most lethal bombs and then missiles with nuclear warheads. The government advised citizens to prepare bomb shelters or places to survive the blast and be protected from the ensuing radiation. In cities and towns, there were signs directing you to the nearest "Fallout Shelter." Thoughts of where to go if a bomb fell were always with you. A novel written by Nevil Shute in 1957, "On The Beach," was widely read and discussed as we pondered our future in this crazy world.

The armed conflict to stop the spread of communism in Korea had ended in an uneasy truce. The creeping spread of communism in Eastern Europe, Asia, and Central America was a major concern, and the fall of Cuba and Castro's alliance with Russia was a definite "line in the sand" threat.

The probability of combat was not a major concern to those being drafted and enlisting in the military at that time. Many of us just wanted to put in our two years so that we could get on with our lives. I had planned to join the Navy so that I could "see the world."

The pervasive fear of imminent attack was counterbalanced by the carefree image left by the fifties. Television shows such as *Leave it to Beaver, Father Knows Best, The Andy Griffin Show, Milton Berle,* and the music of Lawrence Welk and Elvis Presley reflected "the good old days." It seemed that everyone went to church and leaned heavily on their faith to cope with the uncertainty of tomorrow.

The Peace Corps may have been born out of the need for us to act, to do something to relieve the anxiety we felt. An opportunity to serve in a positive way to calm our unsettled world.

The induction notice left me confused and shocked. I tried to call the draft board in Modesto. They informed me that they only met once a week and were closed until next week. The office gave me a number in Sacramento to call, which told me my only option was to appeal at the next draft board meeting, but I must report as ordered.

I called the Peace Corps and was lucky to connect with an administrator who assured me that they would not intervene with Selective Service boards. It was a major concern that men did not view Peace Corps as an alternative to military service. In fact, the military could draft people while serving their terms as volunteers.

Rushing back to the campus, I was able to meet with Warren Smith, Dean of Agriculture, and make arrangements to take two of my finals on Saturday, while other professors waived my finals for the current cumulative grade. On Sunday, we drove to Hughson, and on Monday morning, I reported as ordered. Carol decided to join her family on a camping trip to Yosemite.

A Greyhound Bus took us to Fresno, where medics gave the potential draftees a quick physical exam before we joined other inductees for the trip to Fort Ord. After bunk assignments, they issued our boots and uniforms and informed us that we would be sworn in at the Mess Hall after dinner.

"Inductee Carl Murry, please report to the sickbay," the PA announced.

"Oh no, what have I done?" I thought as I searched for the Medical Office.

The Doctor had an X-ray on a screen beside his desk as I entered. He pointed to a chair and asked me to have a seat. "Mr. Murry, how important is it to you to join the Army at this time? I see that you have recently injured your ankle and are still getting cortisone shots."

"Yes, sir. I broke twelve bones when I crushed my ankle between a couple of cars, and I just had some screws taken out last winter."

"It appears that you may have limitations during your training, and unless you have reasons to serve now, we would like for you to wait a year before joining."

"Actually, sir, my wife and I were scheduled to join the Peace Corps in July and would really appreciate a two-year deferment, if possible."

"Yes, I think that would be in the best interest of both of us. Please report to your CO, and he will make arrangements for your return home."

Stunned, I found my CO in the Mess Hall and began the process of checking out. Even though I knew I would serve two years on my return from the Peace Corps, it would be worth it. The army would pay me, and Carol and I could start our family while I was serving.

On arriving in Modesto, I called my folks for a ride home and learned that Carol had joined her family in Yosemite. There was no way to contact them, so I drove up and surprised them. The looks on their faces were priceless!

Two days later, we returned to Cal-Poly and hauled our trailer home to my folks' place for storage. Since we had a

Volkswagen Bug, my folks came down with their pick-up to tow it, and that was another adventure.

The Peace Corps seemed happy to hear from us and immediately sent us information and tickets from San Francisco to the University of Minnesota for July 6, 1962.

TRAINING AND SELECTION

CHAPTER 5

Pre-Service Training

To: Carl and Carol Murry

From: Peace Corps, Pakistan, University of Minnesota

Subject: Training Schedules:

Carl: Arrive — July 7 before 4pm
Induction and Briefing — July 7-8
Formal Training — July 9 - Sept. 9
Camp Training — Sept. 9 - Oct. 5
Home Leave — Oct. 6 - Oct. 15
Departure — Oct. 16

Carol: Arrive — July 7 before 4pm
Induction and Briefing — July 7-8
Formal Training — July 9 - Sept. 15
Home Leave — Sept5 - 24
Departure — Sept. 25

Report to Bailey Hall, University of Minnesota, St. Paul Campus (just off Cleveland Ave). Housing, meals, and $2.00 per day will be provided. Your mailing address will be:

Peace Corps Pakistan Project
Bailey Hall, Room 116
St. Paul Campus, University of Minnesota
Minneapolis, Minnesota

Training syllabus and additional information will be available on arrival.

Airline Tickets for departure at 11:15 on July 6 are enclosed.

A phone call regarding the difference in training schedules assured us that our schedules would be the same.

To make sure we were on time for our flight, we decided to go to the Bay area a day early. Dad and I went to the Giants and Dodger game at Candlestick while Carol and our moms went shopping. After a seafood dinner at Fisherman's Wharf, we went to Carols' grandparents' home in El Cerrito, and my folks returned home. Early the next morning, July 6, Carols' parents drove us to the SFO airport.

The airline delayed our flight because of an oxygen leak, and we sat on the runway for over an hour nursing our anxieties. We changed planes and took off for a stop-over in Denver and then on to Minneapolis, arriving at about 7:30 pm. Our taxi ride from the airport to Baily Hall cost $4.15.

Hot, muggy, green, lush, and lots of beautiful red brick buildings were some of our main impressions as we checked in at Bailey Hall and received our room assignment on the second floor. The married ladies used the bathrooms on our floor, so the men went up to the third floor, where the single men stayed. The single ladies were on the first floor.

The Syllabus outlined our course of study, which went from 8:00 am to 9:30 pm each day, with Saturday evenings and Sunday mornings open.

Saturday, we completed registration, attended orientation, toured the area, met with staff and fellow

Summary of Classroom Hours			
COURSE	HOURS	COURSE	HOURS
Language	240	Personal & Public Health	50
Area Studies	60	Physical Training	50
American Studies	30	Technical Studies	100
World Affairs	30	Peace Corps Orientation	20
Communism	20	Overseas Orientation	20
Total Hours 600			

trainees, and participated in a large press conference. Sunday afternoon, we had a conducted bus tour, which included St. Paul, the state fairgrounds, capitol buildings, Minnie Ha Ha Falls, Como Zoo, Mississippi River, and beautiful green rolling hills and parks. We enjoyed a large "Welcome" banquet with several guest speakers that evening.

On the first day of training, staff bussed volunteers to the main campus for physicals, dental exams, and psychological testing. In addition to the exam, I had a consultation with an orthopedist regarding my crushed ankle and if I would need further care. They would keep me under observation during training. The dentist visit was new to me as I had never seen a dentist before. The interns at the School of Dentistry discovered nine cavities and treated them without the use of Novocain. Our immunizations began with Tetanus and Typhoid shots, followed by nineteen additional injections including Plague, Typhus, Cholera, Yellow Fever, Flu, Polio, Smallpox booster, Rabies, Gamma Globin and Diphtheria.

Language class launched us into our vigorous training schedule. Our instructor used Arabic to demonstrate the articulation of sounds that we would use. Without a specific assignment, Carol and I were enrolled in the Punjabi class. Other classes were Sindi, Pushto, and Bengali.

Most of us suffered from the after-effects of the immunizations, which added stress to our physical and academic performances. The deselection process began with registration and was a constant presence each day of training.

On Friday, a week after our arrival, we finally discussed our project assignment with Dr. Luther Pickerel, University Coordinator, and Kingston Berlew, Country Director, Pakistan. My assignment was to work on a four-thousand-acre government demonstration farm with twelve acres to use at my discretion for experimental plots, demonstration plots, and research. They allotted us a two-room house in a nearby village but expected us to design and build our own mud-brick home on site. Carol would conduct homemaking demonstrations, assist in a nursery, work on community development projects, and perhaps do volunteer work in a nearby hospital. The assignments stunned us as Mr. Fawcett, Peace Corps Recruitment, had assured us that we had jobs in our respective fields, and we had refused other programs to join this one. They apologized and said they would search for a better placement. The seed of Peace Corps "flexibility" was firmly planted.

The following Friday, July 20, recruitment told us that they had not found new assignments. One of us needed to switch to Bengali language classes, so we could help each other catch up if they moved us to East Pakistan. Carol was doing much better in Punjabi, so I switched to Bengali and found it easier for me to articulate. About a week later, Carol also joined the Bengali language group. There was a huge thunderstorm that night, with lightning striking a tree right next to the dorm. The storm impressed me. The following heat and humidity were terrible.

My ankle flared up after a soccer game the following Monday. I bought some tape and began taping it on Tuesday. Little annoyances seemed to occur frequently, no hot water for two days, fire alarms going off in the middle of the night, schedule changes at the last minute, horns honking, unscheduled appointments with psychologists, and group therapy sessions. Occasionally, a trainee would disappear, and the staff informed us that they went home without explanation.

On Tuesday, August 7, we met with Ted Alexander, Agriculture Extension Officer with the United Nations, and Jim Moody, Pakistan Desk Officer for the Peace Corps, to discuss our possible roles in a large irrigation project in East Pakistan called the Ganges-Kobadak Project. Although it did not meet my expectations of being an agriculture teacher, it seemed workable. I would teach and support extension agents at the Baradi Training Center, and Carol would help set-up a Medical Lab at Kushtia Hospital in East Pakistan. On Thursday, the ninth, we joined The G-K training group and at last, halfway through training, had a good idea where we were going and the language we needed to learn.

The nurse assigned to the G-K, Barbara Baden, lived in Minneapolis and hosted a big Bengali party at her house that Saturday night. Our language teacher, Zaharat Ara Anam (Cookie), prepared the Bengali meal and extended the cocktail hour to 10 pm until our food was ready. We were in a convivial mood and had few inhibitions about eating sans utensils. After the meal, cocktail hour resumed with singing, dancing, chugging contests, and profound discussions. Staff reminded us that cocktails were not acceptable or available in Pakistan. The next Saturday night, the group partied at a bar on an island on the Mississippi River called the "Golden Garter."

The survival camp in Puerto Rico provided survival skills to volunteers posted in remote rural areas. There was a backlog of groups waiting for training, and Peace Corps decided that it would not be necessary for me to attend. Instead, they modified survival training components, or in some cases, dropped them from the pre-service training programs altogether. Since many trainees had never camped or spent a night outdoors without facilities, staff organized a weekend camp-out for Saturday, August 25.

Peace Corps bussed the volunteers to a large park on the St. Croix River in Wisconsin. Divided into groups of eight to ten, they provided us a blanket, water, and candy bars, assigned groups two Boy Scout leaders, and we hiked about a mile to a camp area. They assisted us in creating shelters, starting fires, finding edibles, cooking over a fire, proper outdoor toilet etiquette, and offered other helpful advice. We had gathered blackberries for a cobbler in a Dutch Oven, and a person brought in a couple of fish and a bunch of hot dogs for us to cook. Late afternoon, a float-plane landed nearby, and shortly after, Avis, a fellow trainee from Minneapolis, and her boyfriend came to the camp with two pizzas and marshmallows. The boyfriend said he would have brought a case of beer but thought that might be pushing it a little. Avis asked if anyone needed anything that she could bring back in the morning and took off for her date. We all agreed that there are different levels of survival and that we had a lot to learn.

That night, we taught the two leaders and four of our group how to hunt Snipe while we roasted Marshmallows. It was cold, and the ground was hard, but we survived.

On Sunday, September 2, after intense language study, five of us hired a taxi to take us to the Twins Stadium to watch the Minnesota Vikings play Johnny Unitas and the Baltimore Colts. Alan Page and the Vikings defense were excellent in beating the Colts 24-13. The following night, we went through a back gate and enjoyed the State Fair, which abutted the St. Paul Campus.

Volunteers called September 6 "Bloody Thursday," the final day of the selection board meetings, and everyone was nervous. The recruiting offices had deselected eight of the original eighty-five trainees during our training, and thirteen more would leave before noon that day. It crushed me when I received an envelope that morning and learned that my selection was on hold pending my background clearance. Two of the deselected trainees were able to return and inform us that they were appealing the decision. We later learned that they were unsuccessful, and our number had dropped from 85 to 64. Morale was low for the final week. Our last immunization that Tuesday was a huge shot of gamma-globin, which left a knot the size of a large walnut and a big pain in my ass.

Testing, interviews, travel information, and several guest speakers occurred during our last week. Ms. Lily Christy, Peace Corps Travel Desk, helped with logistics, and Charles Vetter, Peace Corps Administrator for the University, challenged our abilities to remain apolitical, and Warren Mason demonstrated how to party on our last night of training. We departed Saturday, September 15, for a ten-day home leave.

CHAPTER 6

Getting There

The ten-day home leave was a whirlwind of tying up loose ends and projecting our needs for the next two years. Peace Corps allowed up to forty pounds of luggage, and we could ship one hundred pounds by sea freight in a footlocker or small trunk. The challenge of projecting needs for toiletries, birth control, clothes, cartons of Marlboros, etc., was somewhat overwhelming, but we found that one hundred pounds were plenty. (If we had only known what we were getting into.)

My parents were wonderful. Storing our trailer, adopting our Irish Setter, helping sell our Volkswagen bug, giving us rides, and being so helpful in general. We greatly appreciated the help because we all knew dad wanted me to stay home and farm, and my Mom could not understand why we would give up the comforts and risk our lives. For Dust Bowl emigrants from Texas and Oklahoma, it might have seemed like we were leaving for a two-year journey to Mars.

Our departure to Pakistan was 5:00 pm on Tuesday, September 25, from New York. We were happy to learn that we would fly out a day early and spend the night in the city before our departure. It would give us a chance to see some sights in the "Big Apple" on Monday afternoon and Tuesday.

By the time we got to our hotel, it was evening, and we were exhausted. Art Sipma and Barbra Baden, fellow G-K volunteers, were there and told us that Denis Doris, a West Pakistan volunteer who lived in the city, recommended a great Irish pub to meet for eats and drinks. They were heading there, so we joined them. Several other volunteers were there, and we ended up staying there until almost 2:00 am. The combination of a late night and the time change meant we didn't wake up until nearly 10 am. We had time to walk around and see Times Square and the Empire State Building before returning to the pub for lunch. It was then time to head for the airport for our 5:00 pm departure.

The Pan Am Clipper was a four-engine prop especially chartered for our group. The pilot took off to the South East over the Atlantic and made a slow turn to the North while climbing and occasionally dipping the wing so we could see the skyline of New York and the Statue of Liberty. It was silent as we ascended, each of us filled with our thoughts. Some may have been similar to mine. What am I doing? Will I return? Two years is a long time!

As we leveled off, there was a thunderous pop from the opening of a champagne bottle, and someone yelled out, "Well, here we go!" A stewardess announced that as soon as the seat belt sign was off, we were free to move around the cabin and help ourselves to free drinks, sandwiches, snacks, and any goodies we could find in the galleys and that they would help us find whatever we needed. Soon, our neckties, suit coats, high heels, and assorted apparel littered the seats. There was an area mid-plane near the exit doors where the airline had removed a row of seats on both sides of the aisle, and a poker game began. It was interrupted a couple of times by turbulence but continued all night.

We arrived in Shannon, Ireland early in the morning to refuel and change Clipper crews. Most had just gotten to sleep and were not interested in getting off. Word spread that we should not pass up this chance to purchase good Irish whiskey at the duty-free shop, so some of us staggered off to buy liquor and pee without being jostled around. In a more sober moment, we might have realized that there was plenty of alcohol available on the plane and that we would not be able to bring alcohol into Pakistan legally. However, the duty-free shop had a battery-powered shortwave radio that became a highly valued purchase for us.

Wednesday morning in Ireland. Everything seemed so green and moist, the air fresh and clean. There were some delays, but we soon left for a six-hour flight to Rome. The sky was clear except for some clouds over Paris, and we circled Rome three times while picking out landmarks before landing for refueling and a crew change. We had about three hours to walk around. It was sweltering! Re-boarding our beloved Clipper that evening, we felt numb and looked like Zombies and were happy to curl up in our seat for an overnight flight to Karachi.

Thursday morning, shortly after 8:00 am, we touched down in Karachi, West Pakistan. Mostly sober, we put on our ties, suit coats, and other formal apparel and said goodbye to the Clipper and its crew.

After several hours in customs, we joined together for a welcoming ceremony with national and local dignitaries with lots of speeches and press coverage. The staff served lunches during the introductions. Since about half of our group would be staying in Karachi for their assignments, those of us moving on spent some time with goodbyes and well wishes. Afterward, we boarded a bus to take us to rest houses, deposited our luggage, and took a sightseeing tour and a trip to the beach, where we had an opportunity to ride some camels.

BOOM! The first stages of culture shock struck like lightning as we toured a huge resettlement area. The heat, humidity, smells, and poverty were nothing I could imagine and assaulted our weary senses. A dead camel blocked our lane, and people swarmed around our bus until our driver could arrange its removal. With the delay and expected traffic, we would be late getting back to dinner at 7:00 pm. Our guides presented the option to skip the beach and get back a little early to the rest house for a shower and downtime. The vote was unanimous, and we arrived back at the rest house about 5:00 pm. The luxury of a cold shower and the opportunity to lie down flat for a short time overrode our disappointment of not having the opportunity to see the beauty of Karachi and its beautiful beaches.

Immediately after lying down, there was a knock on the door by a man selling newspapers. "No, thank you!" A few minutes later, another knock – a boy selling peanuts. We decided to ignore the next knock and did so for a while, but it was persistent. I opened the door.

An old man with a big white beard and a little toolbox stood outside. "I hotel service sahib; I come in," he said. Thinking he needed to do some repairs, I let him in. He pulled out a chair, "You sit here," he instructed. He knelt in front of me, took a hollowed-out cow horn from his box, and reached for my foot.

"Oh, no, my feet are just fine," I blurted out. "Thank you, but no thanks." I tried to show him out.

He shook his head and looked puzzled, "Service, no cost, just tip," he said as he left to our relief.

Without much time left before dinner, we laid down again, only to hear another knock. "Hey, how did you guys like the pedicure?" Terry inquired. Laughing, we opened the door and discussed the day's impressions until dinnertime. After dinner, there was a short meeting and instructions to load up on the bus for the trip to the airport.

Our overnight flight was on Pakistan International Airways (PIA) and departed at 11:00 pm for Dacca. At sunrise, we were flying over a huge body of water with lots of little green islands, and I was surprised that the plane was beginning to descend because I could not see land big enough to land on. It was near the end of the monsoon season, and all the rivers were full.

On Friday at 7:00 am, we finally arrived in Dacca, East Pakistan. A welcoming committee greeted us on the tarmac as we disembarked. Once again, we tackled a myriad of forms and procedures to clear the customs rituals and gathered in a hall for an official welcome and breakfast. At the end of our briefing conducted by the in-country staff, they divided the new volunteers into three groups. Staff escorted our group (The G-K) to an ancient wooden-sided bus that looked like an old Model A. Behind the anachronism, a multi-colored Lorrie hauled our luggage. We continued our journey through Dacca and down to the ghats (docks) at Narayangaon to the paddle-wheel steamer that awaited our arrival.

I wish I had the vocabulary to describe how

Pak II volunteers arrive in Dacca September 28, 1962 at 7:00 am

overwhelming this experience impacted me. First, we traveled for five days in the same clothes (suit and tie) and had not slept in a bed since New York. The heat and humidity were suffocating. Burning charcoal, sewage, mildew, and unidentifiable odors overloaded my western sense of smell. Being the center of attention for the mass of humanity that continually flooded around us, pointing, reaching to touch me, smiling, laughing, begging, and speaking a language that I could not understand, was a bit unnerving. I had trouble processing my feelings and had the urge to be alone and cool, if only for a minute.

Before lunch, we stopped at the ghats of Narayangan on the Burri Ganga River and began to transfer to the paddle-wheel steamer. In-country staff supervised the transfer of luggage, helped us locate our second class area on board, and explained to us procedures for eating, sleeping, and

This steam driven paddle wheel boat provided an overnight Trip to the train station at Faridpur.

the differences between the three classes. First Class was on the top deck and included overnight cabins with W/C, dining hall, deck lounge, and attendants. Second Class was on the main deck and included bunks in a dormitory area, communal W/C, and cafeteria-like food service. Third Class was a passage with sleeping allowed on the rear deck or below in the cargo area. We were allowed to travel Second Class or Third if we preferred.

The steamer departed around 3:00 pm and traveled downriver to Chandpur, where it would turn upriver on the Ganges and continue overnight to Faridpur. We would arrive around 10:00 am, hopefully with enough time to catch a train to Kushtia.

Finally, we changed into casual clothes, separated

ourselves from the crowds, and tried to communicate with the Bengalis on board. They taught us to use the greeting "Adab" because we were Christians, but we quickly changed to the Muslim greeting of "Salaam Alekum," as most people expected it. Throwing out some of our vocabulary words and seeing where they would lead was fun. While only passengers were allowed on board, young boys (6 to 8 years old) would swim out, climb aboard, and dive for pennies (pices) that passengers threw into the river. I remember one little boy holding my pant leg and begging me to take him with me to be my son, promising to be good and work hard. Despite the excitement and the fantastic river views, the lure of a horizontal bed to stretch out on won out, and I turned in just after sunset.

On Saturday morning, the whistle from our steamer alerted the residents of Faridpur of our arrival around 8:00 am. We were able to get our luggage to the train station in time for our 10:00 am departure to Kushtia. The steam-powered trains run on coal and also have three classes of travel. First Class is generally a compartment with seats that make into beds and a little basin and water. Second Class provides you with an individual seat and a small table. Third Class permits you to get in or on the third class car, which may be equipped with bench seats and handhold bars and is very cheap. The best way to describe Third Class is to imagine riding the subway at rush hour with the passengers carrying chickens, goats, sacks of meal, fish, sugar cane stalks, and whatever. I remember standing face to face with an old lady in a burka while the child she was holding was peeing on my shoes.

Two and a half hours later, we arrived in Kushtia, where our team leaders Tom McMahon and Dan Scheer, who were

Peace Corps Volunteers from the PAK l group, met us. We loaded the luggage into the blue jeep, and we took cycle rickshaws a little over 2 miles to the Baradi Training Center.

We slept two people in a room. Our quarters had two rope beds, a small table, and two chairs. A conference room doubled as a dining hall, and a separate building provided two W/Cs' and a bathing area. We met in the dining hall for our first meal and an orientation briefing. At the briefing, we received our schedules for the next four weeks of in-country training and "housekeeping" information for our stay at Baradi. Staff informed us that most of our $75.00 per month allowance would apply to our first month's room and board at Baradi.

Peace Corps had planned a tour of the area following the orientation, but we were able to convince Tom and Dan that it would be in everybody's best interest if we could stop moving after our six days of continuous travel. We retired to our rooms to strip down, lay on our wooden beds, and watch the little Tik Tikies (lizards) chase each other around on our walls and ceilings.

ASSIGNMENT

CHAPTER 7

East Pakistan

Pakistan, a nation separated into two parts (East and West wings) by over a thousand miles of India, was created in August 1947 out of the Muslim majority areas of British India and the contiguous princely states. A republic and member of the British Commonwealth, Pakistan is the world's sixth most populous country and the largest Muslim nation in the world, with a population of approximately 92 million, 86 percent are Muslims.

East Pakistan, a land of rivers, subtropical climate and monsoon seasonal agricultural patterns, is about the size of the state of Louisiana and a population 3 times greater than California and is situated at the head of the Bay of Bengal. It is surrounded by India except for a small part of a border with Burma. It is a vast delta formed by the Ganges, Brahmaputra, and Meghna Rivers and is virtually void of aggregates.

About 96 percent of East Pakistan's 47 million people live in rural villages. It has two cities with a population over 100,000 and a population density of over 900 per square mile, one of the heaviest in the world. Rice is the main crop and staple food and Jute is the main cash and export crop. Yields per acre and per man are low, for some crops among the lowest in the world, due primarily to land fragmentation, dependence on seasonal monsoon cropping patterns, and unawareness of improved agricultural techniques, particularly irrigation.

The above description was from our training syllabus (1962) and, of course, the country has changed considerably since then. In 1972, a war of independence resulted in the creation of the nation of Bangladesh, replacing the name of East Pakistan. Many names have changed – Dacca became Dhaka, the rupee became the Taka, etc. I will be using names that were in use when I was there. The population is now around 165 million, and California's is around 40 million. East Pakistan is about the same size as Louisiana, which has a population of less than 5 million. I will include some of the reports I wrote and excerpts from letters that I wrote home in my descriptions.

I should point out the lack of natural resources in the country. Located on a river delta fan, there is no rock or aggregates to use in construction. To compensate, there are many brickyards. Workers break the bricks to a gravel size for road construction and concrete work. One of my favorite images is of old men sitting under tattered umbrellas breaking bricks into aggregates in front of an elaborate sign proclaiming: SITE OF FUTURE ATOMIC ENERGY PLANT.

I should note that cyclones or hurricanes cause huge losses of life and property each year. Losses of up to 500,000 lives have been recorded from a single storm.

Map of East Pakistan

CHAPTER 8

The Ganges-Kobadak

The Ganges-Kobadak project was undertaken by the East Pakistan Water and Power Development Authority (EPWAPDA) under the guidance and technical advice of the Food and Agriculture Organization (FAO) of the United Nations. This is a combination irrigation farming, drainage, and flood control project, the first such in East Pakistan, and seeks to develop a pattern of agriculture which is not dependent upon rainfall. The project will supply irrigation water from the Ganges River to an eventual area of 1 million acres in the Kushtia, Jessore, and Khulna Districts, and drain off surplus monsoon water and control flooding through a series of drainage facilities. The project is currently in its First Phase, irrigating 130,000 acres.

The introduction of irrigation farming and drainage into an underdeveloped area requires an effective extension service to demonstrate the use of irrigation water to farmers and teach them improved agricultural methods and water management. Unless the tradition-oriented farmers of East Pakistan can be converted to new irrigation methods and improved practices, much valuable construction and planning could be rendered useless or underproductive. Realizing the importance of extension services, EPWAPDA established an agricultural branch in 1960 to carry out extension service. It also set up two demonstration and research stations at Amala and Benerpota to determine optimum water use and cropping patterns under the conditions of the region, and established a training center at Baradi to train extension agents. Fifty Baradi-trained extension agents and six extension supervisors are now in the field.

The extension phase of the project is proceeding rapidly and has shown favorable results to date, but as water becomes available throughout the Phase One Area, the need for agricultural and irrigation extension, research, training in minor irrigation construction, and water management work will greatly increase. To help meet these needs, the United Nations Food and Agriculture Organization has assigned, since 1960, a small team of specialists to the Ganges-Kobadak Project. Additional personnel are needed however, and the Peace Corps has been asked to help fill the gap in trained manpower. The prospective Peace Corps Volunteers will be assigned to the project through the FAO and will work with the specialist of FAO and EPWAPDA.

The team of Peace Corps Volunteers (PCVs) which will be assigned to the Ganges-Kobadak Project (G-K) will consist of agricultural extension workers, agricultural-irrigation field teachers and demonstrators, agricultural research workers, and workers in irrigation management. These PCV's will have backgrounds which stress practical experience and field work. All Peace Corps Volunteers in the G-K Project will be assigned within the Phase One Area under the coordination of a Volunteer Team Leader.

The project description above comes from page four of "The Peace Corps Training Program Syllabus for Pakistan," University of Minnesota, July to September 15, 1962.

CHAPTER 9

Our Team

Sixteen volunteers were assigned to the project including Barbara Baden, our team nurse and assistant at the Kushtia district hospital, and Carol Murry, who was to set up and operate a medical laboratory at the Kushtia district hospital and teach English.

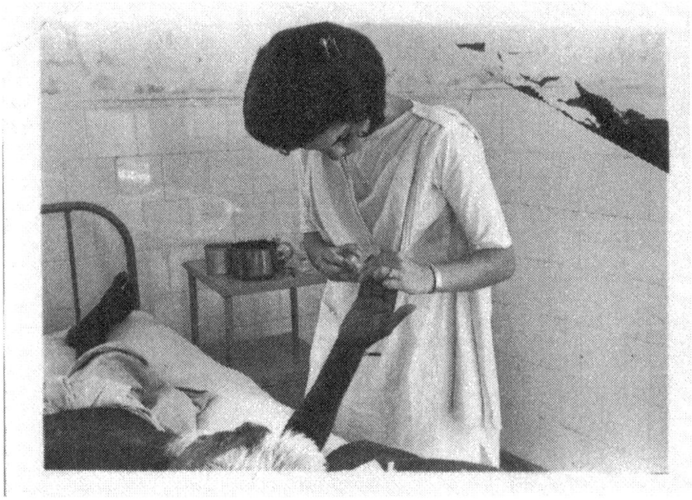

Carol drawing blood from a patient n Kushtia District Hospital where she started a medical laboratory.

The team members are:

~**Barbara J. Baden**, 12-15-1932, Minneapolis Minnesota. Central High School. R.N., College of St. Catherine's, St Paul, Minnesota. Eight years nursing experience. Has traveled extensively in Europe. Served with the Red Cross as a volunteer nurse.

~**Carol J. Murry (Mrs.)** 1-11-41, Denair California. Hughson High School. B.S. in Biology, University of California, Santa Barbara. Member of Modesto JC Farmettes. She has worked as a laboratory technologist trainee.

Walt Winant and Willis Hanna were stationed at the Amala Research Station.

~**Walter M. Winant**, 11-13-1937, Brentwood, Maryland. Northwestern High School. B.S. in Soils, University of Maryland. Field Research on tobacco, corn, soybeans, hay, and wheat. Course work in Meteorology, Geomorphology, Botany, Chemistry, Mathematics, and Physics. Graduate work in Soil Chemistry.

~**Willis E. Hanna**, 9-9-1938, Honeoye Fall, New York. Avon Central High School. A.A.S., Alfred State Tech. B.S. Agronomy, University of Georgia. U. Army Clerk and Chaplains assistant School. Worked on a farm for many years.

Grant Wells and Harold Meyers served as engineers and water quality inspectors at Berhamira and Kushtia respectively.

~**Grant De Witt Wells**, 5-14-1937, North Adams, Michigan. North Adams High School. B.S. Agriculture Engineering, Michigan State University. M.S. in Agriculture Engineering, Cornell. Active in 4-H and FFA. Member of American Society of Agriculture Engineers. Assistant at Cornell in Mechanical Drawing class with occasional lecturing.

~**Harold D. Meyer**, 2-15-1933, Gerton, North Carolina. Edneyville High School. B.S. Geological Engineering, North Carolina State College. Electrician's Mate, US Navy. Laboratory assistant in Mineral Research, North Carolina State College. Hydraulic Engineer, US Geological Survey, 1959-1962.

George Randal and Ken Jaeger, extension agents at Norapara.

~**George D. Randol**, 4-7-1942, Cantua Creek, California. Tranquility High School. One year Animal Husbandry, California Polytechnic College. One year History at East Central State College, Oklahoma. Member of 4-H and FFA. Experience in livestock farming.

~**Kenneth D. Jaeger**, 12-9-1924, Idaho Falls, Idaho. Idaho Falls High School. US Army in Germany 1944-46 and Japan 1945-46. Studied farm welding and machinery repairs, cattle feeding, and dairying at veterans association sponsored school for two years. Managed 400-acre farm intermittently for ten years. Experience in irrigation farming.

Terry Bixler and John Lehecka, extension agents at Swastipur.

~**Terry J. Bixler**, 9-18-1942, Waynoka, Oklahoma. Waynoka High School. Completed two years of Agriculture at Northwestern State College. He has worked on a farm for several years and was a member of the Future Farmers of America.

~**John A. LE Hecka**, 3-12-1942, Rock Hill, South Carolina. Rock Hill High School. Two years of Mechanical

Engineering at Clemson College. 4-H member for two years. Has been insulation helper, a welder, and a pipefitter's helper. Experience in citrus farming and irrigation.

Art Sipma and Marvin Horst, extension agents at Poradaha.

~**Arthur Sipma**, 9-7-1932, Ripon, California. Born in the Netherlands and graduated Escalon High School. US Army in Germany. Member of 4-H and FFA. Has lived on a dairy farm and is experienced in irrigation work, repair of farm machinery, livestock, and grain farming.

~**Marvin E. Horst**, 9-3-1935, Windsor, Colorado. Boulder High School. Certificate from Rutherford Automotive Institute in IBM operation and bookkeeping, Dallas, Texas. Studied Agriculture at Colorado State University for one year. Member of 4-H for eight years, and 4-H leader for three years.

Ray Priday and Tom Foley, extension agents at Mashon.

~**Raymond W. Priday**, 4-1-1944, Terrebonne, Oregon. Redmond High School. President of local Future Farmers of America. Has lived on a farm all of his life and has experience with beef cattle, irrigation procedures, and all types of farm machinery. Member of 4-H club.

~**Thomas L. Foley**, 1-26-1943, Clinton, New York. Holland Patent High School. Member of Future Farmers of America since 1958 and County President 1961-1962.

Pete Hansen and Carl Murry, extension agents at Baradi.

~**John P. Hansen**, 5-31-1939, Fresno, California. Washington High School. B.S. in Agronomy, Fresno State College. President of Agronomy Club, 1962. Has experience in cotton and alfalfa farming and in irrigation work.

~**Carl R. Murry**, 6-5-1939, Denair, California. Hughson High School. A.A.S. in Agriculture, Modesto Junior College.

B.S. in Fruit Production, California Polytechnic College. President of FFA. Member of California Young Farmers and Crops Club. Has lived and worked on a farm most of his life.

These initial assignments changed as circumstances and project needs evolved.

CHAPTER 10

Getting Started

The first week of training at Baradi Training center seemed intense, with so much to learn and soak up. We started at 7 am with language classes for most of the morning. During breaks, we would go outside and play games like London Bridges, Drop the Hanky, Duck Duck Goose, etc., with the children or walk around absorbing our new environment. It was hot and humid with the monsoon season winding down, and the afternoon rains were refreshing.

Playing London Bridges with children at Baradi, September 1962. In the center Barbara (left) Carol (middle) Carl (right).

Project personnel presented their respective departments, explained our assignments, and how we would be working together. FAO officers included Mr. T. Alexander, Mr. W. Blackie, and Mr. Erdal Ozbelin. WAPDA officers included Mr. F. Haque and Mr. D. Ahmed. Our Peace Corps personnel included – Kingston Berlew, Country Director for Pakistan, Paul Slawson, Associate Director for East Pakistan, and Jay Crook and Robert Terry (EIL), Technical directors. Thomas McMahon and Dan Scheer were Team Leaders for our project.

A part of our orientation was to become familiar with the postal system, banks, markets, transportation, cooking and eating, and other daily concerns. We learned that it was not wise to mail envelopes as all mail is subject to inspection, and postmaster Sahib will open them to ensure the contents are acceptable and confiscate anything questionable or perhaps valuable, and stamps are expensive. The Aerogram only costs 60 paise and can be inspected without opening. The postmaster often opens incoming mail, and a volunteer shouldn't even think of sending cookies or cigarettes. We subscribed to the Asian edition of *Time* magazine, highly-valued for newsprint pages (as opposed to the slick shiny ones) in lieu of TP. The magazine was gone through page by page with a marker pen to cover up exposed cleavage, legs, and other provocative skin. Frequently, postmasters ripped out entire pages.

Our monthly allowance was US $75 per month for each person, which we deposited in our local bank and withdrew cash as needed. The budget was more than adequate, and we were able to put some aside for vacations and trips. All volunteers received the same amount, and I assume that the volunteers living in the cities would have to budget more carefully due to their ability to access more goods and services. Prices were rarely preset, and we bargained for most commodities. The Rupee was equivalent to about 20 cents, with 5 Rs equal to USD$1.00. There were two systems of coins: the decimal system (100 Paisa to a Rupee) and the British system of 16 Anna per Rupee. The Anna coins had different shapes (square, lobbed, serrated, hole in the middle, etc.) so blind persons could count them.

Preparing meals was a full-time job, and PC expected us to hire a cook. The cook would rise early for the markets. In Kushtia, there was a market every day for the basics, and locals held specialized markets on designated days. Mondays and Fridays you could buy goat meat. Saturdays were for beef. The fish market was on Wednesday and other days as available. Shoppers bought chickens live when available. Most villages had a market once a week. Without refrigeration, the majority of the meat had to be cooked or prepared soon after purchase. I often saw chickens with their legs tied together, feeding around a home until needed – this ensured fresh poultry at the dinner table. Locals ate meals with fingers and drank from a bowl or cup. Banana leaves sometimes served as plates.

Asian toilets consist of a concrete basin with a drainpipe and a raised, red brick-sized footrest on each side. Water in various containers, from plastic pails to bronze pitchers, were available for washing up and flushing. Showers consisted of elevated containers with a spout or, in most cases, a large container with a cup to dip and pour over yourself. The most common method of bathing is a dip in a pond (Pookur).

Cultural practices that we needed to know were that locals punished stealing by cutting off the offender's right hand at the wrist. It is standard practice to always use the left hand for washing yourself after using the toilet, and you should never use the left hand to give anyone anything, as it is very offensive. Locals expect visitors to know this if they speak any Bengali.

The training would usually break around 5 pm for exercise and free time. The poker game, which started on the airplane, resumed during this time slot. Paying my dues, I learned to play poker by losing half of my monthly allowance that first week. Knowing when to hold them and when to fold them was expensive.

The first week of our four-week in-country training at Baradi Training center was about adjusting to our new time (Detroit is halfway around the world from Dacca). Adapting to the heat and humidity, the sounds and smells, sharing our space with Tik Tikies, assorted bugs, livestock, and many other people. It was about realizing how inadequate our language skills were and trying harder. It was about appreciating our new friends, co-workers, and the unique culture that engulfed us.

On Saturday, we participated in a field trip through our new town and to a village where we talked to the people in our broken Bengali, ate raw sugar cane mixed with fresh bananas, and watched the grinding of the canes. Located in jungle-like areas, the villages are almost impossible to drive to. That evening, we observed a big Hindu celebration as we walked around downtown Kushtia, and I bought my first Lungi, a piece of cotton cloth approximately 3x4 foot sewn to form a tube and worn like a skirt, and a long white shirt.

During the second week of training, PC dispersed volunteers to job sites to settle in, get acquainted with our areas, and continue language training with our co-workers. Staff assigned Carol and Barbara to the hospital in Kushtia, and they were in the process of building a two-bedroom house for us in the G-K Colony. We temporarily lived in the Government Rest House, about two hundred yards away from where our permanent house would be. The rest houses were similar to Temporary Officer Quarters on a military base. Authorized personnel can stay for a nominal fee, and they provide meals. "Boy Howdy!" We felt like we were walking in tall cotton with our rope beds, tap water in the toilets, fans, and occasional electricity.

The organization assigned Pete Hansen and me to Baradi, which is about a mile from town. We spent some time at Baradi looking into the areas available to us for gardens, demonstrations, and discussing possible plans with Wakil and Abul, our co-workers, and fellow extension agents for our site. We visited five or six of our villages on our bicycles. The paths through the jungle were narrow, muddy, and filled with ruts and potholes. Often, we had to carry our bikes over bamboo bridges and swampy areas. Many of the villages had specialties such as weaving, linseed grinders, sawing lumber, candle making, and sewing. Wakil would introduce us to the headman in each village and local men of note.

Carol and Barbara went to Dacca for training during this week, and when they returned, we decided to remain living at the Rest House and ride out to Baradi for training sessions. I finished smoking my last pack of Marlboros and started trying out local brands such as Ramna, King Stork, and even country "Bidi's." King Stork was a little bigger and cheaper but often had weevil holes in the paper, which made them difficult to draw.

Our third week of training featured Robert Taylor, a PAK I volunteer, working to develop agriculture cooperatives in Comilla. He is a Cal-Poly graduate from Knights Ferry, CA and has been successful in creating a cooperative to market dairy products, including butter and cheese.

Our circle of friends multiplied, and volleyball and cricket teams both invited me to play. They were talented teams, and my play humbled me. Although, I really whacked a couple out of the park with that flat cricket bat. There were bars on our windows but no shades or curtains, and there seemed to be a crowd watching us all the time. It is easy to empathize with monkeys in a zoo. In a crowd, children will stroke the hair on your arms to see what it feels like. Being a woman without the covering of a burka and a foreigner as well, kids followed Carol around like she was the pied piper, hoping for an interaction.

The fourth and final week of training found us a little impatient and eager to start our jobs. After lunch one day, I smiled as I watched a mother hen and her six chicks cleaning up under my table while a cow watched at the window, and two small goats wandered through the door. Birds nervously tend their nests in the roof, and Tik Tikies chase down bugs on the wall.

Feeling restless, I decided to take a stroll through the sugarcane fields. I came upon an old man feebly hacking away at a log with his crude axe. He looked so weak and frail, and an urgent need to help him overcome me. In my broken Bengali, I offered greetings and persuaded him to give me his axe. With power and confidence, I swung the axe and, in that single blow, broke his axe handle in half. It was strange how my entire Bengali vocabulary suddenly vanished. Looking him in the eyes, using my non-verbal skills, I shrugged my shoulders, turned, and walked back through the fields carrying only my shame.

Our final day of training ended with a sigh of relief and a modest ceremony as we prepared to settle in at our assigned sites. A shopping trip to downtown Kushtia provided our basic supplies. The mostly paved main street was wide enough for vehicles to pass each other. Small lanes paved in brick with a small concrete gutter on one side housed the majority of the shops. The gutter was mostly open and used for cleaning and urination. The shops reminded me of the booths at the Fair. Some were large enough to walk into, but most rose about three feet, and the owner sat inside surrounded by his goods. You would point to something and ask, "Khoto Dom" (how much)? He would give you a price, and you say, "Boro Bese" (too much) and then try to reach an agreeable amount.

Shopping on the main street of Kushtia.

The Muslim women keep purdah, which means that they do not go out in public, and mostly stay in their compounds (homes). When they do come out, they usually wear a full-body, tent-like dress with a net opening for the eyes called a burka.

My first haircut was, fortunately, uneventful. No blood and a little hair left around my ears. Myself and four others had our first bout of diarrhea; we suspect it was one of the snacks we purchased.

ON THE JOB

CHAPTER 11

Here We Go

It was finally time to apply all of my recently obtained scientific agriculture knowledge and my "lifetime" of production experience to help the people of East Pakistan to increase their production and stomp out world hunger! My starting goals included:

1. Set up an irrigation committee for our T4K ditch to discuss the best distribution system, cooperative crop plans, schedules, and production concerns.
2. Start a garden at Baradi Center.
3. Select a farmer for demonstrating fertilization, pest control, and other management practices.
4. Explore the feasibility of starting a "Chasi Club."
5. Develop bulletin boards for villages.
6. Investigate teaching an agriculture class in a Kushtia secondary school one day per week.
7. Look for possible citrus rootstocks for citrus budwood.

My counterpart, Wakil, was capable, helpful, and easy to work with. We began by riding our bikes and walking around theT4K farmlands, where land fragmentation presented our first major obstacle to flood irrigation. The land plots varied in shapes and sizes, some as small as 100 square feet and others an acre or more. Farmers would have to cooperate.

An examination of the canals and ditches revealed new obstacles and concerns. There are three main canals, Kushtia, Ganges, and the Alamdanga. They are about one hundred yards wide, including the "borrow" ditches on either side, and the top of the banks are leveled off and graded to provide roadways. Bridges span the main canal at intervals of one to four miles. The secondary canals branch off of the main canals and average about thirty yards wide with paths on the banks. The tertiary canals branch off of the secondaries. The farmers are responsible for water distribution from the Tertiaries. We label the canals accordingly – S4K is the fourth secondary from the Kushtia main canal, and T7K is the seventh tertiary from that secondary.

Baradi Farm receives its water from T6K and T7K from S1K and is operational. We were to help develop an irrigation plan for T4K and discovered the intake gate for this canal had been constructed below the check dam instead of above, and the only way to get water in it was to pump it. Wakil said that sometimes a landowner would pay the construction crews to alter plans to save his land. On reporting it to our supervisors, they told us that they were aware, and the corrections were on their repair list.

We became aware that many such corrections were to be made, and many of the farmers were irate at the project and its representatives. Crews took a considerable amount of the farmers' land to construct the ditches while not compensating them fairly. Construction had severed traditional paths and roadways, requiring long trips to bridges to move around. They disrupted natural drainage. Farmers frequently cut canal banks to net fish. Residents identified the extension overseers as representatives of the project, and locals confronted and occasionally threatened us.

Our first Irrigation Committee meeting for Baradi village occurred on Nov. 27, 1962 at 3:30 pm. Wakil, Pete, and I joined Abdul and waited until 4:00, as only two farmers joined us. We visited until 4:30, and two more farmers joined us. By 5:00 pm, the committee had a total of seven farmers present. Chairman Babu Nermal Kumar Shaha asked us to wait a little longer because he sent two young men out for something. They returned 15 minutes later with two chairs for Pete and me. Squatting beside chairman Shaha was an old man who seemed familiar to me. Pete and I felt embarrassed that they went to all the trouble to bring us chairs and tried to relinquish them to the chairman and the older farmer.

"Please accept our hospitality," the chairman insisted. "My father tells me that he met you in a field near Baradi about a month ago."

"Oh yes, I remember, and I want you to know that I am so very sorry for breaking his axe," I replied with embarrassment.

"He tells me that you have a good heart and will need our help," he said with a smile. "It is a busy time for us cutting Aman and Boro rice and sowing Grame and Wheat where we can."

The Baradi irrigation committee meeting at the training center. With chairman Shaha's father on the far left.

I recorded the minutes of our first meeting in my journal to give you an idea of the farmers' concerns. I copied the minutes below as I found them [sic]:

~Kam'd Asol Ahmed felt that drainage in T7K was one of the biggest problems. The water is too deep to harvest and too wet to sow winter crops because some fishermen have dammed up the drains near Mirpur, the Colanga Dam is backing up water and a sandbar has built up on the Gori River.

~Abdul Hamid was concerned with a beetle that has been eating Gram plants during the night but they are afraid to apply spray because it could poison the straw they feed to the animals.

~Meser Sheik was concerned about the encroachment of Water Hysen and suggested we spray them before they get too bad. He did not think composting would

be practical but was interested in purchasing fertilizer from Baradi Center. We were not aware that Baradi had fertilizer for sale but would look into it.

~MD Seray Mollik would like to plant Wheat but the seed is too expensive and the Agriculture Loan Office required collateral of land and animals. Much of the land is farmed by sharecroppers who do not have collateral.

~All of the farmers seemed to be interested in having a monthly nightschool to share problems, learn new information, and play some games. We should set one up in January , after harvest. They would like to restore the old Baradi Grammar school as a meeting place.

~Other interests included getting Orange and Pomelo buds to be budded on the wild local lemon trees, composting, animal production and the US Government sponsoring visits to America for village farmers and not managers that don't really farm.

We served tea, and the meeting adjourned at 6:15, with the next meeting to be in early January.

The hospital does not have a Lab, and Carol has received a grant to set one up. She has been busy ordering equipment, including a microscope, centrifuge, chemicals, slides, and just about anything she needs for a basic lab. There is a "Compounder Shahib" that has a mortar and pestle to mix up medicines. A unique feature of the operating room was its location in the front of the hospital nearest the street. It had two large barred windows so that family and interested passersby could observe surgeries and treatments.

Carol agreed to teach English in a primary school from 7:30 to 9:30 each morning and then work two shifts at the hospital from 10:00 to 1:00 and from 2:00 to 5:00. She became sick after the first week and worked part-time for three weeks with flu-like symptoms. During this time, there was an outbreak of cholera in several villages around Kushtia, and over four hundred people died. So many could have been saved with simple IV's. It was around mid-November that we were both taking worm medicine at the same time. She had Whipworm, and I had Pinworms.

After work, we participated in community activities. I was playing volleyball, soccer, and cricket with different teams. On the cricket team, I played wicket-keeper and loved smacking the little ball around with the flat bat. Carol attended a lot of teas and social get-togethers.

One Saturday afternoon in early November, there was a huge political rally on the soccer field next to the Rest House we lived in. A friend came by that morning to advise us to stay inside during the rally. There was a big conflict brewing with India, and the USA was giving aid and weapons to India, and there might be some angry people who would want to confront us. We set up a place on the roof to hide and observe. We were nervous as a helicopter landed, and a politician addressed the crowd over loudspeakers while they chanted. Mobs are terrifying.

A college invited us to attend a Bangla Play one evening. It started around 7:00 pm and lasted until 12:30 am. Someone stole my bicycle during the play, and when my friends found out, they formed a big posse and found the guy who stole it and turned him over to the police. I would have never found it without their help. They would have cut off his right hand in the village, so spending time in jail wasn't so bad.

One morning, Wakil rushed in and said he was sorry, but a great sickness was in his village and that he must return to care for his wife and little girl. Pete and I asked if we could help, and he said we must stay away from the village, but to please ask Allah for mercy. The next morning, he came again and told us his wife had died and that his baby daughter was sick also. That evening, Carol told us that a cholera epidemic was spreading fast in the Gugia/ Barkada area. Warnings posted informed people to stay away. In the village, residents butchered a black goat, stuffed its hide with straw, and mounted it high on a bamboo pole to warn others of the cholera. It is heartbreaking to think how something as simple as providing IV's to replace fluids from vomiting and diarrhea could have saved so many people. Wakil also lost his child, one of more than four hundred in that outbreak.

On Thanksgiving Day, Mr. and Mrs. T. Alexander invited all of the volunteers to their house in Bheramara for a meal. Wow! What a special treat – fried chicken, potatoes, gravy, cornbread, and pumpkin pie. They also had peanut butter, cheese, and butter that they get through a special deal in Dacca. The Alexanders are from Goldendale, Washington and are employed by the United Nations, Food and Agriculture Organization (FAO). He is also a square dance caller.

Pete and I finished surveying the canals and were feeling depressed that so many of the canals were inoperable. We set up a Boro Rice demonstration plot and arranged for delivery of government-subsidized fertilizers to Baradi. We encouraged several farmers to plant wheat but abandoned the line planting method. We tried fastening a funnel to the handle of the plow with a tube to drop the seed in the plow furrow. The farmers did not like to carry the bag of seeds, and it was distracting while trying to keep the right amount of pressure on the plow.

The cattle are weak, and most operate by voice commands only. There is no harness or ropes, and the yoke, a piece of bamboo, is just placed on the necks with the plow attached. The farmer usually has a small bamboo stick about two feet long to help guide the animals from the rear. Most of the time, he directs them by voice commands similar to the way we used to drive a team of horses with calls of "Gee, Haw, Whoa" and mouth clicks. The plow is a tree limb or root shaped to a point with a vertical handle attached. If you point the plow point too low, it will dig in, and the cattle will just stop. Pete and I both tried our best to plow a course, but it must have been our foreign accents that caused our failure. The farmers certainly enjoyed the show of ineptness, some laughing to tears.

Water Buffalo are the Peterbilts and John Deeres of the country. They provide the power for hauling the big loads and mulching the flooded soil for transplanting paddies. They are docile and pampered by grateful owners. As a bonus, they provide huge manure patties to dry for fuel.

Frustration and disappointment are beginning to erode our enthusiasm. So much of what I expected to be doing will not be possible. Teaching and training sessions are always postponed or cancelled.

Most of the canals are non-functioning. We abandoned plans because of failed deliveries (seed, fertilizers, pumps, citrus bud stock, and equipment). Our surface freight has not arrived. Our house, which was supposed to be done by the end of training, is dragging along. Language fluency is still not up to my expectations, and everyone seems to say 'yes' to everything to spare your feelings.

Responsibility is too often relegated to God. "Allah will provide."

"It is the will of Allah."

"Don't worry; it is in the hands of Allah."

It seems like everything can be done tomorrow. If tomorrow ever comes, we will work ourselves to death.

Add in some culture shock and homesickness with the coming Christmas season, and the need for a rally seems obvious.

CHAPTER 12

Loving Dacca

A great shout out to our wonderful Peace Corps staff for setting up a conference in Dacca for Christmas! Eight of us left Kushtia via train on the 23rd to catch the Paddle Steamer to Dacca. Not surprisingly, there was a mix up in our reservations, and no beds were available. Boat staff were able to find some cots for Carol and Barbara. The rest of us sat up in the Galley and played poker all night. We docked in Narangange about 9:00 am and took motor rickshaws 15 miles into town.

To our delight, we discovered an Italian restaurant for lunch, and they served beer. We had been on site for nearly three months and had not yet been "to town" and did not realize all the luxuries Dacca had to offer, especially, beer. Since it is basically a dry country, we did not know that it was available. Murray Beer is brewed in West Pakistan and comes in 32-ounce bottles. Also, Lion and Eagle Beer, brewed in India, are available but are more expensive. We later learned that we could buy distilled alcohol from a "medical shop" if we registered as alcoholics and received a permit. Some of us registered, but the liquor's quality was disappointing. The hooch came in various bottles with a stopper covered with black wax or tar, varied in clarity, and tasted like rubbing alcohol. We were able to use it as a disinfectant. I guess we were not 'real' alcoholics.

With a delightful after lunch glow, we arrived at the Peace Corps Hostel for a short tour and a meeting with staff, fellow Pak II volunteers, and some Pak I short-timers. Visiting and sharing experiences was truly refreshing and uplifting for us. The afternoon ended with a spirited co-ed softball game, which we lost 21 to 16. After dinner, we built a large bonfire and sat around singing Christmas Carols. For many of us, it was our first Christmas away from home. Volunteer Jack Jordan sang "O Holy Night," and it was so beautiful and powerful that it has remained one of favorite memories of all time.

We attended an Anglican Church service at 11 pm and then returned to the Hostel for a midnight dinner followed by a party, which ended as dawn began to break at 5:30 am.. We crashed until noon.

The staff had arranged for some of us to stay with American families working in Dacca for a couple of days. Our family was just a man and his wife. He worked with the United States Overseas Mission (USOM), and they lived in a gated compound near the embassy. We felt privileged to enjoy soft clean beds, hot water, good food, cigarettes, radio, TV, and wonderful company. Most government employees also had access to military services, such as the PX, commissary, and APO mail.

On Christmas night, we attended a large dinner party in the compound that featured a fantastic array of food and drink. We visited with members of the American community that seemed very interested in our experiences.

I was able to make some valuable contacts that could assist us with our projects. This is where I began to learn about other American services.

The next two days were spent contacting USOM, USIS (US Information Service), CARE (Cooperatve for Assistance and Relief Everywhere), Asia Foundation, Department of Education, Department of Agriculture, and the Peace Corps Office. USIS said that they may be able to loan us movies with a projector, screen, and generator. CARE would like to give us some small moldboard plows to demonstrate farming techniques The Peace Corps gave us a trunk with about two hundred books to read and share and informed us that many volunteers had received their surface freight, so ours should arrive soon.

We departed Dacca on the 28th via the Paddle Steamer, and this time we had bunks to sleep on. We arrived back in Kushtia on the 29th and checked on our house as we wanted to move in before the New Year.

CHAPTER 13

New Year, New House

Batteries recharged, we returned to Kushtia planning to move from the Rest House into our G-K house that was supposed to be ready mid-October. An overseer and two laborers' were digging a drainage ditch when I went over to check it out. They had hoes and baskets to dig the trench. The overseer said the house would be ready when they finished the trench. I told him that I could help and got a shovel, which is much faster than the hoe/basket method. I joined the laborers in the trench, and the overseer became very distressed and asked me to stop. I just smiled and said, "It's OK; I don't mind working." He then ordered the men out of the trench and joined me in digging and was clearly upset. We stopped, and he explained that it was embarrassing for a man of my class to be joining these men of the lower class and that he was trying to save me the embarrassment by joining me. I wanted to argue with him but realized it would be better, for several reasons, that I stop and apologize.

The Maintenance Department assured me that the house would be ready next week, and I informed them that

Our house in Kushtia which we moved into in January of 1963 and it still wasn't finished when we left.

we would be moving in the next day, December 30 and that I would be happy to assist with any finishing details. There were several modifications that I planned to make anyway. One of them was to build a tank on the roof over the toilet to supply water for a shower and washing up, shelves, and a mirror. A large clay pot or similar container holding water with a dipper was normally used for washing up.

Households typically obtained water from a tube-well with a hand pump to fill buckets. They then transported the buckets to the kitchen or bathroom. I fit the pump with a hose bib and a hose that we could use to fill the tank on the roof and enjoy a gravity flow shower.

The brick/stucco house had four rooms, a small kitchen area with coal-burning fire pit, and a kerosene stove. Barbara stored medicines in a tiny kerosene refrigerator provided to us. It was off-limits for other uses. A large table served for food prep and a basin for washing up. There was also a screened cabinet, about two feet by four feet, for food storage. Adjoining the kitchen was a dining/sitting room with a large table and several chairs. It also had a ceiling fan.

The two bedrooms had rope beds, an El Mira (closet cabinet), a ceiling fan, and a toilet between the two rooms. The toilet had a door to each room with slide latches on both sides. The ceiling fans would have worked, but there was no electricity.

Peace Corps provided cooks while we were living in the Rest House. Now, we had to hire our own cook and give some guidance on the menu. It was interesting that most of the cooks we interviewed had been employed by British or missionary families, and most went by biblical or English names such as John the Baptist, Luke, Daniel, Paul, or Mark.

The temperatures dipped down during the winter months (December through February). We had recently experienced temperatures down to 40 degrees (F) overnight. We would bundle up with a blanket and seek out the morning sun to keep warm. There was no indoor heating. So, I thought I would build a fireplace in the sitting room but, thankfully, realized that fuel would be a huge problem. Locals fuel cooking fires with coal, dried dung patties, and precious wood scraps, and to burn them for warmth would be an impractical luxury. Some affluent families did use Kerosene heaters to warm their rooms.

We enjoyed improving our home with landscaping, gardens, and personal touches as time went on.

CHAPTER 14

We Can Do This

January 1963. We began the new year with renewed energy. Wakhil and I met with our irrigation committees, constructed and distributed our bamboo and burlap bulletin boards, and reviewed our curriculum for the ten-day training program on fertilization, seed selection, treatment, pest control, and irrigation.

On January 11, Carol and I traveled by train to Bheramara to meet with Mr. Alexander to review the outline of my ten-day in-service training program for the extension agents that was to start on the 14th. He informed me that the 14th was Police Sports Day, and we should postpone the workshop one day. We also needed to condense it to three days because of budget and other concerns. The Extension Officer wanted to start a Tractor Demonstration program and asked that I be in charge of the Kushtia area.

Mr. Alexander had asked that Carol come up for the meeting because he had prepared her a surprise birthday lunch for her with a cake and gifts of a little brass bell and a big jar of Peanut Butter. We listened to music tapes, visited, and shared stories of home and family. They were very dear people, and we had a wonderful time.

The Police Sports day was a lot of fun, and just about everyone participated in one way or another. There were relay races, talent contests, songs, dances, stick games, sporting events, and many games. One game consisted of each participant given a clay pot and bamboo stick (about two feet long) and instructed to break each other's pot. – the last person to preserve their pot wins. I was doing well when the college headmaster told me my pot, which I was holding behind my back, was cracked. I brought it around to check it, and he quickly broke it.

One of the requests from our Irrigation Committees was to arrange for chicken vaccinations for fowl pox/AE. We were able to obtain vaccines from the Department of Agriculture and an adequate supply of syringes. Setting dates at Gugia, Jella, Barcada, and Noapara, we would demonstrate a wing web inoculation and leave materials with the village headman for future use.

My upset stomach and flu-like symptoms led to some pretty severe diarrhea and some concern from Barbara. After two days, she arranged for me to fly to Dacca. Doctors diagnosed and treated me for Amoebic Dysentery, and I returned three days later, weighing several pounds lighter (under 150 lbs). I worked in our garden, close to home, for the next couple of days.

Ramadan began on January 27, and physical work slowed considerably as everyone fasted all day, including water. Some of the more devout would not even swallow their saliva.

Carol and Barbara started a program to visit pregnant women in the villages, and we arranged visits through our irrigation committee's recommendations. They also fielded questions about birth control and supplied an intrauterine pill when requested. One of our friends came to me one morning very concerned about his wife.

"She took a pill memsahib Barbara gave her, and it tasted very bad, and she has a lot of foam coming from her mouth," he reported.

" Oh, sorry, Khalil, the pill is not supposed to be taken by mouth," I explained.

The CARE (Cooperative for Assistance and Relief Everywhere) organizations sent several moldboard plows to Baradi to demonstrate to the farmers. Most farmers would not use them because their cattle were not strong enough to pull them, and the turned soil was more difficult to prepare for seedbeds. Farmers with teams of water buffalo could use them for ditching and making raised seedbeds. The Tractor Demonstration program was of interest to our committee members to prepare the Aman rice fields but would start in March/April.

I was sick again, and Dr. Goldstone asked me to come into Dacca for further testing at the hospital. He confirmed that I had a serious amoebic infection, and he prescribed new antibiotics. Associate Director, Paul Slawson, arranged a lunch with our Ambassador to update him on the progress of the G-K Project and invited me to accompany him in driving to the agriculture conference in Mymensingh. The drive took about five hours with many primitive ferry crossings. I was able to learn more about the various Peace Corps projects and agricultural developments in the country. The conference was well organized, informative, and helpful. We took the train back to Dacca in time to attend Jack and Rachel's (Jordan) wedding before returning to Kushtia with four quarts of Murray Beer.

Our surface freight finally came on February 16. It had arrived in Chittagong in December and only taken two months to travel the last 150 miles (five months total). I was happy to get Marlboros and razor blades. Some of our group never did receive their surface freight.

Booster shots for Typhus, cholera, rabies, gamma globin, smallpox, and a TB test resulted in another sick day. Barbara let us choose between a small gauge needle for a longer, less painful dose or a larger gauge that was much quicker but with a more painful injection of the thick GG serum. We were all on our best behavior and extra kind to Barbara on shot days because she could choose when to sharpen her needles on the little marble slab. *Gee whiz, why didn't they have disposable needles back then? ... Hmm, do you suppose? ... Nah, she wouldn't do that!*

Since work had slowed down, we decided to take a long weekend to visit Calcutta, which was only 75 miles away by train.

CHAPTER 15

Calcutta

It is only 4 hours by train and costs R7.00 or $1.40 to go to Calcutta. However, there is a five-hour layover at the border to pass customs and immigration inspection. There is a real problem with the black market money exchange, so there are thorough personal searches of shoes, shirt sleeve cuffs, hatbands, etc. The official rate of exchange is R5 to USD1, but you could get 10 to 15 Rupees per dollar on the street.

After ten hours, we arrived at the Dum Dum train station and hired tongas (horse drawn rickshaws) to take us to the Salvation Army Hostel. It was quite late when we arrived, but we got a shared room for three nights with three breakfasts for about $5.00. The persons we shared the room with worked night shifts, so we had to be out of the room by 6:00 am, but we could leave our travel bags in the room. They were nurses, and we visited at breakfast before they went up to the room.

A troop of small monkeys (maybe spider monkeys) would come in the windows around daybreak and wake us up. We went for early morning walks before breakfast, and I was surprised to see men with two-wheeled pushcarts picking up the bodies of the people who had died on the street during the night. They would wheel them down to the burning ghats on the river Hooghly to be cremated.

The slums, shanties, and extreme poverty we experienced in the outskirts gave way to beautiful wide streets, ornate buildings, upscale shopping, and historical sites. The shops had a huge array of carved ivory, exotic knives and weapons, silks, silver and gold ornaments, and tourist items for low prices. We chose to spend our money on great food, steaks, hamburgers, french fries, cokes, ice cream, milkshakes, good cigarettes, and beer.

The Queen Victoria Monument was very impressive. We also went to the India Museum, Zoo, and several other attractions. We were able to see two movies – "The Longest Day" and "Romanoff and Juliet." We enjoyed ourselves immensely.

There was a Methodist church about two blocks from the Salvation Army, so we attended on Sunday morning and realized how much we missed church services.

Beggars congregated in our area and around any transportation hubs. Most were severely disabled, maimed, and pitiful. It was overwhelming and heart-wrenching. People told us that there were beggar villages, where people would purposely starve or maim children to be more effective in begging. It's so disheartening to contemplate the degree of poverty that would even consider those acts as options. This experience weighs heavy on my heart and conscience even today.

With full stomachs, fond memories, smiles on our faces, and, perhaps, guilty consciences, we returned to Kushtia on the 25th of February, the last day of Ramadan and the beginning of Eid. Eid is the biggest holiday of the year. Similar to our Christmas, it is a time of visiting friends, giving gifts, feasting, and goodwill. We received many Eid Cards from our friends.

CHAPTER 16

Transition

We spent the Eid Holidays at the end of February and early March on home improvement projects and a "clean up day" at the hospital. Before returning to work, Pete, Carol, and I traveled to Comilla to confer with Bob Taylor on his successful Agricultural Cooperatives. Pete and I also spent some time with a team of Japanese experts on rice production while Carol visited the hospital and Cholera Research Center.

On our return, we found that we had picked up some parasites, probably lice. We boiled all of our clothes and bedding, scrubbed down, and applied some kind of medicinal powder.

Feeling eager to get projects rolling again, we began to feel resistance from our co-workers. Something had changed. The pumps for Abu Gori were not available. The tractor program had not restarted, and I was unable to locate the driver. There was low attendance at our meeting in Gugia, and the bulletin board at Barcada was gone. On my return from Barcada, my dysentery flared up again.

Two days later, I left for Dacca via airplane from

Isurdi and went to Holy Family Hospital for IVs and tests. Doctors determined that my liver had been infected, and I had amoebic Hepatitis. I remained in hospital for a week. The first few days were foggy, but on the fourth day, I got a roommate. He was a tea planter from Sylet who had broken his leg, and every afternoon his wife would come to visit him with a six-pack of San Miguel beer, which he was happy to share with me.

While explaining our project to my new friend, I realized that one of G-K's big problems was communication. We were spread out over twenty miles and had a general idea of what each other was doing but little feeling of sharing and working together. Perhaps I could coordinate a newsletter each month, and it would be good to get together once a month. I also thought a great deal about my dreams about poverty after we visited Calcutta.

On Friday, Our Peace Corps doctor, who usually checked with me in the morning, stopped in as we were enjoying our second San Miguel.

"Is that beer you are drinking?" he asked.

"Yes, it is a very good Filipino brew, and we have an extra one for you if you would like to try it," I replied.

"Oh, no! You are not supposed to have any alcohol with a liver condition. I just stopped to let you know you are being released tomorrow morning, and I have some medication for you to take with you."

"Sorry, Doc, I didn't know. It certainly won't be a problem in Kushtia."

I returned to Kushtia on March 24, and on the 25, we had a joint meeting with our overseers and the new chief of Agriculture Extension, Mr. Huq. He planned to transfer extension workers to the lower end of the project, including our volunteers. To travel so far away and start new programs when they had just got started disappointed many.

During the day, I gathered information from the volunteers on their projects and asked several of the agents I knew to send a brief report on what they were doing so that I could prepare a newsletter sample. I also invited all of the PCV's to spend the night to play a poker game, talk about our projects, and discuss the reality of what we were doing.

The positive reports included Will and Walter from Amla Research Center, where they had a defined job and latitude to contribute their expertise. Harold and Grant also had specific tasks, which were needed. Carol was making real progress that was appreciated by the personnel at the hospital, and her English teaching class at the G-K school delighted her. Barbara was busy tending to volunteer health and helping at the hospital. Art Sipma had invested his time learning the language of Bengali with his co-worker and visiting tea shops regularly and had earned much respect for his efforts. He and Carol were our best Bengali speakers.

Most extension workers had mixed success but were feeling much frustration, probably me more than the others.

Jay Crook served as an assistant Peace Corps Director for both wings. He came to Kushtia to see if he could assist with our job definitions. From upper New York, his father was a minister, and he had converted to the Muslim faith. Being fluent in Arabic and Bengali, he easily gained street creds with our co-workers and became a good friend.

On March 7, at a Master Farmer meeting in Kirthi Nager, the farmers presented their irrigation plan for a double crop on March 12. The overseer had submitted an indent (request), and it was approved ten days earlier, and the canals were operational. On March 10, a 400-man crew from the Engineering Division began minor repairs by filling in borrow pits and destroying the outlets we needed for distribution.

This enormous set-back devastated me, and I dreaded facing those farmers whose trust we valued and needed.

CHAPTER 17

Go Home, Or?

"OK, that's it, we are just wasting our time here, and I am feeling so frustrated that I feel like going home!" I ranted.

"Nobody said it would be easy, and maybe you are setting your expectations too high. I really enjoy my students, and progress at the hospital is slow, but it is progress," Carol responded.

"I know some of the other extension volunteers are feeling like I do, but it's difficult to generalize the feelings of others. I will try to explain my reasons for feeling frustrated and considering giving up."

Culture shock. There is an obvious culture shock on first encountering a new environment and culture, and it can feel overwhelming at times. There is a deeper shock, which occurs four to six weeks later, when the novelty has worn off, lifelong support systems are missing, physical adaptations become a burden (shower, shave, toilet, bed, lights, fans, etc.), health and wellbeing are a struggle, and the feeling of being appreciated is questionable.

Goal-oriented. My motivation was to increase food

production by teaching and showing these folks how to grow more and better crops. Making friends, learning about their culture, religion, fears, hopes, and aspirations were fringe benefits of striving to achieve my real goal.

Work ethic. Growing up on the farm my, dad taught me that when something needed to be done, you did it. Timeliness is often critical. The amount of time you spend on a job depends on how long it takes you to finish it, not what time it is. When irrigating, you might get the water at 11 pm and end at 5 pm the following day, work 30 consecutive hours during harvest, work 14 to 16 hours, 7 days a week for an entire month. So, I am motivated to "get 'er done" and have little tolerance for putting things off.

Real-world experience. My world growing up was not diverse in regard to race or culture, except for my friends who happened to be Italian, Portuguese, or Mexican. Religious diversity seemed overwhelming at times, with squabbles between the Baptist and Methodists and the many protestant denominations, not to mention all our differences with the Catholics. Graft and corruption are present in our society, but I never had to deal with it. In other words, I was very naïve, and my world was growing so fast I could hardly keep up.

Health. The toll of parasites, dysentery, infections, and fevers had worn me down. I felt guilty for missing so much work and embarrassed by feeling so weak. My weight had dropped from 175 to 145.

I needed to evaluate the many jobs I worked and set new goals. The answer to the question, "should I go home?" was a definite "No!" There were so many needs that we could help with, and we needed each other's support. We decided to get together once a month to work on a community project, play poker, and have a party.

We were sitting around sharing a loaf of bread and picking out the flies that had been baked into the bread when Barbara asked, "What do you think our Moms would say if they could see us eating this bread?" We all burst out laughing.

Carol and Barbara created this Jingle which they loved to tease us with:

"We drink whiskey with the best of them,
Rum with the rest of them
And Tea with the G-K men!" (pinkies extended)

CHAPTER 18

Adapting

We all began looking for ways to be more helpful and effective in our jobs. This was the beginning of the busiest time of the year – harvesting winter crops and preparing the fields for the broadcast planting of the Aus Rice crop.

We prepared the first edition of our newsletter, "The G-K Extension News," with the assistance of Nuru Zamman and Dan Scheerer. The Chief Extension Officers, Mr. Huq and Mr. Ahmed, approved and distributed it in early April.

The covers of the first and last copy of The G-K Extension News.

Through my contact with the United States Information Service (USIS) in December, I was able to borrow a movie projector, screen, generator, an assortment of films from their office in Rajshahi, and show films at our irrigation committee meetings. We called it the Cinema Project and rotated the supplies around to other volunteers to use in their villages.

The first rains had come, and the pressure to complete as much tractor work as possible was building. My workdays were longer and hurried. On Saturday, April 27, I started plowing fields in Mashon at 6 am in hopes of finishing by noon and then taking the equipment to Bheramara for service. Finishing the scheduled plots on time and preparing to leave, Mr. Hossain asked if we could do one more small plot for the chairman of his irrigation committee. It was some distance from the village and difficult to get to. On the way back, I got the tractor stuck and spent all afternoon getting it out.

There were tube wells in most villages to get drinking water. The heat and a lot of sweating made me very thirsty, and we asked for a villager to bring us water. He was gone for a long time, and when he returned with two small jars of water, we hardly minded the awful warm taste of the greenish liquid with wiggly things floating in it.

A team of water buffalo and a lot of bamboo helped us get the tractor out and back to the Mashon Center, where I got my bike and was home by 7 pm.

The next morning, I felt squeamish as I rode my bike out to Mashon to get the tractor. By the time I got to Bheramara, I was sick and asked someone to take me and my bike back to Kushtia. My fever lasted for five days and got up to 105 degrees. After the fever, I rested for two days before trying to work again but returned home by mid-day, too sick to continue.

A few days later, Terry Bixler broke his leg, and the Peace Corps asked me to accompany him to Dacca for medical attention. Paul Slawson, APCD, wanted to meet in regard to the G-K project while I was there. The Airport at Ishurdi was about 30 miles away and usually had two flights a day to Dacca. DC-3 puddle jumpers serviced it, and the runway consisted of perforated steel panels from the WWII era. It was faster but more expensive. However, since I was traveling on a request from the Peace Corps, it was on their dime.

We missed the afternoon flight and decided to return to Kushtia and try for the morning flight the next day. Our bus to the train station broke down, and we missed the train and ended up taking the train to Dacca via Mymensingh, which involved four hours by train, two hours on a ferry, and the remainder of the night to arrive in Dacca at 7:30 am the next morning.

Doctors put a cast on Terry's leg and asked him to stay for observation. Paul Slawson wanted to talk about the morale of G-Kers and if I would consider being the Team Leader after Tom and Dan left the next month. On the way to the airport, I saw an advertisement for Coca Cola, so I stopped to "pause and be refreshed" and buy two quarts of Murray beer to take with me on my flight home.

The extension centers consisted of a small two-room residence and a room for meetings. Initially, the meetings were for Irrigation Committees, but we now referred to them as Chasi (Farmers) Clubs.

There were five or six Chasi Clubs within a ten-mile radius of Kushtia that I had been assisting. The ten-mile bike rides were tiring but reasonable in most cases. When you factored in the sudden thunderstorms and Monsoon rains along with breakdowns, the trip got a little more difficult. One evening after a Chasi Club meeting in Hazarati, I had a blowout on my rear tire and had to push the bike eight miles to get home (about three hours).

Since teaching at Baradi Center was not happening, I felt that my best contribution would be to meet with the overseers each month and assist them in preparing educational programs with lesson plans, teaching aids, social activities for their monthly meetings, prepare and distribute the monthly newsletter, and develop awards or recognition programs to provide incentives for participation. We also discussed a Master Farmer Program.

Easter Sunday, April 14, 1963, was a highlight. Carol roasted a skinny chicken, prepared mashed potatoes, beans, and chocolate pudding. We dyed some boiled eggs with dye from her lab, and Barbara started teaching us how to play bridge. Volunteers Dan and Judy from Rajshahi also visited us.

Boat parties on the Ganges river was a enjoyable way to entertain visiting friends as this trip on Easter sunday.

The month ended with several breaches in the canals, including a huge washout on the main canal. The farmers were irate and protested for two days at the site with sticks, spears, and shovels. They demanded that we turn off the water. In some areas, they cut ditches on purpose to net the fish that washed through.

CHAPTER 19

The Rains Cometh

In early May of 1963, our garden had just begun to produce beans, tomatoes, and cucumbers as the rainy season approached with periodic and unpredictable thunderstorms. Hot, muggy weather would suddenly turn into a violent rainstorm, and a few minutes later, we would be working in the hot, muggy weather again. We quickly learned the value of the large, sturdy umbrellas that everyone seemed to carry.

As the rains increased, so did the numbers of cockroaches, mosquitoes, snakes, and assorted bugs. Small lizards called Tik-Tikies and Geckos thrived and multiplied as they moved around the walls, devouring the abundance of new bug life.

John Leheka and I were returning from Swastipur on our bicycles late in the afternoon of May 13 when we noticed a large crowd blocking the road. Thinking it was some kind of accident, we dismounted, but the crowd seemed very angry and yelled at us.

"Ki hochi bondu?" I asked.

"My brother, we are facing great difficulty asking the proper authorities to do the needful things," a nearby student replied. Another student I knew from playing cricket joined us. He said that we must leave right away and follow them as they cleared a way through the edge of the crowd. We later learned that it was a school demonstration in protest of testing.

The following morning, John and Pete took the Jeep into Kushtia to get some petrol. As they were returning down Main Street, a large crowd blocked the road. Pete pulled over, and the crowd quickly surrounded them, grabbing and pulling on their arms as the mob tried to take the Jeep keys. Others started letting the air out of the tires. John jumped out to stop them. The students assaulted them. As he tried to get back in, they took his hat and shoes and threw them at him. A small kid threw a brick that cut his leg. Anything loose in the Jeep was taken, including some letters that John had just received.

Pete finally got the Jeep started and began driving slowly and gained speed as the mob got out of the way. Shaken, they returned to our house and warned us that we might all be in danger, and we tried to figure out the best thing to do.

Shortly thereafter, the District Commissioner and several police officers arrived and explained that the school expelled 27 students from the school for cheating on their matriculation examination. The students are allowed to take the standardized exam three times in order to graduate to the next level. It was their third attempt, and failure meant their education was over, and the headmaster was responsible. They apologized for the few students causing the trouble. Police arrested ten students and placed them in jail. Most of the town people were ashamed, and the students treated us extra nicely.

One of my goals had been to teach an agriculture class in a secondary school. There are two systems of education. First, villages may utilize elders to teach children the basics of reading, writing, math, and religion. They are called Mulvis, and the teachers establish the schedule and curriculum at their discretion. The British system has a universal curriculum, standard exams, which determine advancement through the levels to the university. Changes to the curriculum cannot be made at local levels. I started an agriculture club after school at Jele Secondary School to introduce projects and FFA activities to interested students. The main interest of the students was to practice speaking English, and attendance was very erratic, so I decided to drop it and put more effort into the Chasi Clubs.

Carol saved the life of a baby the previous Saturday at the hospital. It had a very high fever; its pulse was barely detectable, and its face had turned dark blue. A Doctor had given the baby some medicine, wrapped it in a sheet, and left, telling the mother there was no hope.

A nurse who worked with Carol came to the lab and asked her to come, as the mother was becoming hysterical. Carol unwrapped the child and bathed it in cold water. She sent someone to the market to a special store to buy an icy treat similar to a popsicle and used it to rub over the baby and further reduce its temperature. That night, the baby's temperature fluctuated at around 100 degrees. On Sunday morning, it was down to normal, and Carol was very popular.

She was also very popular at her school, where she had her students writing letters to third-grade students at Hughson Elementary School. Those kids really loved her.

Our monthly meeting and poker game was on May 24

before a meeting with Alexander. Carol became very sick, and Barbara accompanied her to Dacca for treatment. She returned June 1, just after a cyclone hit on the 28th of May.

The cyclone came ashore in Chittagong with winds exceeding 140 miles per hour. It was without much warning as attempts to reach the southern districts by radio were unsuccessful. The loss is somewhere between 25 to 30 thousand people, along with heavy structural damage. In Kushtia, the winds were around 60 miles per hour with very heavy downpour and moderate damage.

CHAPTER 20

Monsoons

We held a birthday celebration right after Barbara administered our booster shots on Sunday, June 2. Pete (5/31), Dan (6/3), and mine (6/5) were all a year older, and Carol baked a cake from a mix that Pete's parents had sent. She gave me a new wallet to replace the one I had recently lost, a box of corn flakes, and a tin of syrup.

Monsoons are cyclic periods of rain and constant misery. When it is raining, you want it to stop. When it stops, it is so hot you just want it to rain again. At times, the patterns are so regular that you can plan your day around them. For example, "Let's leave right after the 9 am rain, have lunch and visit during the 1 pm rain, and then get back before the 4 pm rain."

It is difficult to describe how miserable the heat can be. Hot, sticky sweat drips from all your pores. A bumpy red rash called prickly heat spreads from the neck, underarms, insides of elbows and knees, crotch, and other locations. Prickly rash itches but is painful to touch. Fantasies of a cool breeze prevail.

The heat continues through the night with no cooling. The mosquito netting stifles any hint of air movement. We stripped the webbed (rope) beds of any sheets or coverings that might obstruct air movement. You get up frequently at night to shower or pour water over your head for temporary relief.

The discomfort provides motivation to invent various types of fans or mutual comfort pacts. A person could easily go nine months of the year without any clothing, but social standards require us to make adaptations. Loose, baggy shorts without underwear, flip flops, and when a shirt is required, a large, loose, lightweight cotton pullover that has pockets below the waist. For lounging around, a Lungi (a large tube of cloth) and a singlet work well.

Attendance at the Chasi Club meetings was minimal because of the rains. The interest in the Master Farmer program seemed to be growing, and we talked about incentives for the farmers to participate, including certificates, field trips, medals, dinners, and cash awards. The pressure to expand Chasi Clubs to the lower end of the project was growing.

Because of the rains and a Peace Corps language conference in West Pakistan, we decided to postpone our Chasi Club meeting until August.

Tom McMahon and Dan Scheerer completed their two years of service as PAK I volunteers and were returning home. We held a good-bye party in Bheramara for them. Betsy, Mary Jane, and Jean visited and participated in our work/clean-up day at the maternity clinic at Gopalpur.

Peace Corps held the Language Conference in the mountains of northern West Pakistan at a place called Dunga Gali. Following the conference, we wanted to take some vacation time to visit Kashmir, Kabul in Afghanistan, Delhi, and the Taj Mahal.

You may recall in the chapter on Calcutta, I mentioned that I had some spiritual dreams that I wanted to talk about later. This seems like a good time.

CHAPTER 21

Spiritual Insights

How do we deal with the overwhelming presence of poverty that engulfs us? To look into the eyes of a starving person and walk away, to pry the fingers of a six-year-old child from your arm and refuse to take him home with you, to not wash the snot and flies from a baby's face as its mother pleads for food, to watch an amputee hop along without lending him a hand. How could I do that?

Rationalize, pretend, avoid, dehumanize, make excuses, pray for forgiveness; all are options. After the Calcutta trip, I had frequent dreams of the destitute. In one very significant dream, I was standing at the pearly gates being judged for my actions on earth, trying to defend my lack of charity by claiming that I only had a subsistence allowance and could not afford to give that money away, there were too many in need.

If you were wealthy, would you spend that money trying to help others? How much does it cost you to wipe a baby's face or lend a hand to a cripple? Can you acknowledge the condition and empathize with them rather than avoiding and looking away? You do not need wealth to be generous and caring. How do you judge yourself?

From that time on, I never wanted the responsibility of making a lot of money. What a demanding job it would be to spend it wisely, and I am not sure I could trust myself.

My religious beliefs stemmed from a very narrow and strict interpretation of the bible through the Church of Christ, which my parents enforced with conviction. Carol belonged to the Methodist church, which I joined when I was 20 years old.

The Peace Corps made it very clear that we were free to practice our religion when able, but we should refrain from proselytizing. I decided it would be best to avoid religious discussions altogether because I was not very tolerant of other views.

Working side by side with devout Muslims, their faithful prayers five times per day, and their adherence to the five pillars of Islam impressed me, and I felt we had more in common than I'd thought.

It was much more difficult to relate to the Hindu religion. When I expressed my confusion and revulsion of the many deities and idols associated with it, a friend, who was a student and Cricket teammate, explained that Hindus accepted and valued all religions. Every person has their own path, and it may take several cycles or lifetimes to reach nirvana or union with God.

As a child plays with dolls to learn the role of motherhood, new devotees learn relationships by practice with symbols they can relate to and the stories that teach them the right behavior. I realize that I am overly simplifying things, but my reason for mentioning them was to share that I was being offered personal perspectives that helped me learn and grow.

There were a few Buddhists that aligned themselves with the Hindu community. I understood the story and teachings of Buddha, but later learned a great deal more when I lived in Thailand for three years.

Spiritual awareness and growth is a lifetime gift of the Peace Corps service and strengthens my faith and moral compass.

A feeling of joy built as we looked forward to escaping the monsoons while attending the language conference in the West Pakistan mountains and enjoyed a few days of vacation that July.

CHAPTER 22

Language Conference

The conference was an opportunity for us to reunite with the West Pakistan volunteers we had trained with in Minnesota. We left Kushtia via train to Faridpur, where we caught the overnight steamer to Dacca. This time, our reservations were good, and we got to enjoy a bed after our poker game.

Arriving in Dacca around noon, we had time to do some shopping and try to get our camera repaired as the lens was sticking. We also had a party and a three stooges movie before our departure Sunday morning, June 30, to Lahore.

From Lahore, we flew to Rawalpindi in a smaller prop plane and then boarded two older busses for our final leg to Dunga Gali. The busses were old, with wooden benches for seats. A cold rainstorm turned to hail, and we had to stop in the town of Murree because a landslide had wiped out 300 yards of road and was unpassable.

It appeared that we would have to spend the night in the bus. Someone was able to contact the USIS, and they gave us permission to go up to their building and sleep on the floor. It was about three miles away, and we found a place to buy some bread on the way and arrived at the building around 12:30 am. It felt good to lie down and stretch out, and they had hot and cold running water.

The next morning, we found a restaurant nearby for a nice breakfast of eggs and toast. Murree is a ritzy looking resort town with a lot of amenities. Wouldn't mind staying around for a while, but we hiked the three miles back to the busses.

Dunga Gali is about 20 miles from Murree over the worst road I have ever seen. It was very narrow, muddy, unpaved, and extremely steep. I was truly scared the entire trip. The landslide was about ten miles up the road, and they were still working on clearing it with hoes and baskets as we arrived. It was barely wide enough for a vehicle, with an extremely steep drop on the right side. We got out and watched as the busses crept through. The second bus, ours, slid just a little bit, and the rear wheels were less than a foot from going over. Everyone was taking pictures and fully expected the bus to slide over the edge and roll down the hill.

The quaint hill station resort at Dunga Gali was not what we were expecting. A small village of about five stores, the resort consisted of a large lodge for dining and meetings and small wooden cabins with tin roofs, scattered around the hillside like a mother hen and her brood of chicks.

Beyond rustic, the cabins had rope beds, mosquito nets, two small tables, two chairs, a fireplace, and a commode. There was no water or electricity. Our attendant tended the fire, lit the lamps, brought us hot water twice a day for spit baths, and emptied the commode, so I guess it was kind of plush!

The elevation was about 8,300 feet, cool during the

day and cold at night. What a welcome relief from the monsoons. The mountains have a lot of pines like the Sierras but are very steep, and there are troops of monkeys running around who will throw rocks and pine cones at you if they feel threatened. They don't throw very hard.

The conference was excellent. We chose to study how to read and write Sanskrit. The alphabet consists of 52 characters representing specific sounds, rather than the many blending sounds of English. For me, being able to read signs and papers really helped increase my vocabulary. Of the three languages I have studied, Bengali was the easiest after learning the aspirations, honorifics, and tenses, and I may have reached the FS 2+ level. By far, Thai was the most difficult because of the tonal inflections, where the single syllable 'ma,' may have five different meanings, depending on inflection. Swazi included five clicks, which required practice but was doable for me, except that I didn't use it enough to become proficient.

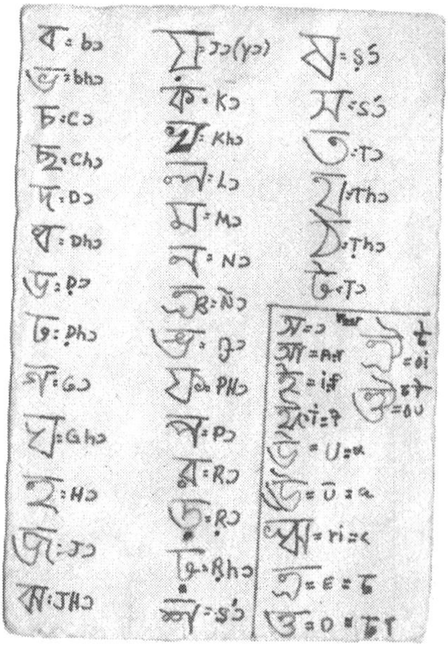

This was my handy reference to the Sanskrit alphabet and pronunciation Guide on the reverse side.

Some of my favorite Bengali phrases included:

- Ki hochi? (what's happening)
- Tash khela hobe (card game will play)
- Ta holay (in that case)
- Ami apnar bhahalo achi (I love you)
- Ba be de bop (exclamation)

Our teachers were professional in scheduling and teaching methods and supportive and challenging in their instruction. On the fourth of July, they cancelled class for a big bonfire with singing and dancing and a "fireworks" display, featuring sparklers and a couple of army surplus flares.

The next afternoon, July 5, the conference gave us some time off to go on a guided hike and mountain climbing adventure. I was excited and looking forward to it when Ken pulled me aside to ask if we were interested in a different adventure that involved a hot shower and drinking beer. We waited until the group left and then walked back down the road about two miles to a tavern with rooms and a bar. There were six of us, and we all pitched in to rent a room, took turns going in for a nice hot shower, and sat around drinking and visiting.

The conference ended Saturday evening, and we took the bus back to Rawalpindi on Sunday. From there, we took another bus to Peshawar to stay with friends on our way to Kabul.

CHAPTER 23

Khyber Pass

After 9 pm, we finally arrived at our friends' house in Peshawar, and we stayed up late visiting. Our bus to Kabul left at 10 am, so George suggested that we go out to the Peshawar Air Force Base and get some food and cigarettes to take with us.

The facilities amazed us. It was like an oasis in a desert. We bought some stuff at the NCO club and hurried back to catch our bus. It was a nicer bus than most, and we could relax a little on the steep winding road to the border at Khyber Pass. Most of our conversation was about the pleasures of the Air Force Base and how nice it would be to go back there.

After completing the customs gauntlet, we went to the bus loading area to wait for our bus to Kabul. There seemed to be more people than a bus could carry, and we learned that the morning bus did not come, and the afternoon bus was late. Not a pleasant prospect.

The bus that we arrived on would be returning around 2 pm, and it was still there in the boarding area. A quick decision was the first step in our reentry to Pakistan.

Fortunately, we found a kind person to help us with our exit/entry stamps and were able to catch the bus back to Peshawar.

George was surprised to see us and understood our decision to return. He suggested some places for us to visit, including the old town and Kohat gun factory for the next morning, and he would take us back out to the Air Force Base for lunch.

Can you imagine our joy in having a cheeseburger, french fries, and a milkshake for lunch? We were in hog heaven! George had to work but said he would come back and meet us for a movie that evening.

The large, beautiful, clean and sparkling pool was surrounded by a lawn with tables and chairs scattered around it. We laid on the grass, ate hot dogs, drank really good beer, smoked American cigarettes, and listened to good old American music from the jukebox.

We enjoyed visiting with some of the airmen stationed there. Most of them did not like being posted here and seldom ventured out from the base. We shared some of our adventures and the sights to see, encouraging them to explore while they had the chance but conceded our envy of their air-conditioned barracks and eating opportunities.

George returned early and found us enjoying a softball game with our new friends. We decided to have pizza and beer and watch TV in the NCO club to wrap up our visit.

With sadness and regret, we said goodbye the next morning, Wednesday, and flew to Lahore to make arrangements to travel to Kashmir. Sightseeing in Lahore was limited and uncomfortable due to the extreme heat.

CHAPTER 24

Vale of Kashmir

Busses were not an option on the washed-out road to Srinagar. However, we were able to book a round-trip flight from Amaritsar. Early Thursday morning, we took the bus from Lahore to Amaritsar and flew on a DC 3 to Srinagar.

Clean, clear, refreshing air greeted us as we disembarked and sought information and transportation. Several wooden buildings that resembled a military base or outpost flanked the airport. The Jhelum River ran through the center of town, with many canals and lakes feeding into it.

The town had a "frontier" feeling to it – wooden buildings with thick sod roofs where goats grazed mixed with ornate mosques and beautiful gardens. We had heard of the houseboats on lake Dal and were able to bargain the price down from R45 to R30 ($6.00).

Ornate boats with fringed canopies, called Shikaras, were taxied us to our houseboat. The luxuriously furnished boat was about 40-foot long with a kitchen, bedroom, bath, and sitting/dining room. Vending boats cruised around selling flowers, toilet paper, books, magazines, food, and

Houseboats and shikaras (taxi) on lake Dal in Srinagar, Kashmir.

items to meet your every need. We bought bread and curry and truly enjoyed the calm tranquility of beautiful Lake Dal.

A flag raised on the bow of a houseboat indicated that you would like a shikara to take you ashore to one of the many tourist attractions. First, we rented bicycles and rode around town, shopping and sightseeing. The Shalimar and Nishat Gardens were on our list of highlights. We ended the day with a hike to a temple overlooking the city.

The next morning, we took a picnic lunch with us on a bus trip to the beautiful Pahalgam valley. Trout filled the streams, but the cost of a tourist fishing license was too much. We enjoyed some interesting hikes before returning to Srinagar.

Water skiing and swimming in Lake Nigeen were the following day's highlights. It was unforgettable skiing around the Lotus blossoms on the lake. Our wooden ski boat had an inboard four-cylinder car engine to power it and was fast and loud. Sharing our boat was an English couple who invited us to join them for dinner and a night of dancing and drinking.

Gulmarg is a famous British resort on the outskirts of Srinagar and has a large variety of facilities and activities to enjoy. There are Polo grounds, Cricket pitches, soccer fields, Tennis courts, swimming pools, gyms, ski slopes, skating rinks, and much more. We chose to rent horses and ride 15 miles through the forests up to the snow line.

Being saddle sore the next day, we ended our stay by visiting handicraft factories, shopping, and walking around town. We flew back to Amaritsar on Wednesday, June 17, and a missionary couple offered us a ride to Lahore. On June 18, we flew from Lahore back to Dacca.

Our flight to Isurdi was unable to land because of a storm, and the turbulence made the white-knuckle trip one to remember. The next day, the weather remained bad, but we were able to land and catch our train to Kushtia. We arrived at our house around 9 pm on Saturday, June 20. It was wet, moldy, musty smelling, and in dire need of cleaning.

Being able to read and write Sanskrit was valuable to me. Signage, ads, newspapers, letters, and other printed material really helped to increase my vocabulary. Good call Peace Corps.

CHAPTER 25

Changes

The following is an excerpt from my monthly report for June,1963:

> *As I understand it, the role of the volunteer extension worker is to be placed in an area with G-K overseers to assist and help them as co-workers. In my opinion this is like throwing a man down a well to help another man out. What we need to do is put a rope in the hands of the volunteers so that they can support the G-K overseers. The type of rope would probably be different in each individual case. For some it may be more authority, access to work shops, seed money, or simple recognition. For me it would be transportation. There is no reason why we must stick to jobs predetermined by persons who did not know the true situation as it exists now. We need to discuss changes with all parties.* [*sic*]

In addition to my monthly report, I wrote the following open letter to the Peace Corps staff:

THE PAGOL AMERICAN IMAGE

Originally, I was gung-ho on the Peace Corps image, pictured as a hard working American who could gain the respect and friendship of people by denying himself of all luxuries and physically working with the common people of under developed countries. This sounded very good in the United States and I suppose it still does to those who are still there.

In East Pakistan, this image pictures a young, crazy American who is unsure of what he is doing. There are educated persons who have an understanding of the American society and ideals and individuals with whom we have gained friendship through personal contact and working relationships, who respect our intentions but not necessarily our methods. To the majority of the people with whom we have no personal contact, we are judged on our actions that often run against their society. Thus we often hear laughing behind our backs and are made fun of because we are known as "pagol shahebs" or crazy men.

We learned through our relationship with the Peace Corps, that a person must be flexible. The Peace Corps image should be defined to fit the individual country. In my opinion the Peace Corps image in East Pakistan should reflect all those typical and important traits set down by the administration such as honesty, sincerity, kindness, willingness etc. but MOST IMPORTANT it should reflect a person who sets out to do something worthwhile quickly, efficiently and completely regardless if it is done on foot, bicycle, or Rolls Royce.

No longer can I agree with the idea that a Peace

Corps Volunteer will be more effective by making himself appear as poor and humble as the average farmer. East Pakistan has enough poor humble farmers, what they need and want is someone who can help them. I am sure they would appreciate a man who can make their life easier much more than an inefficient, powerless, do-gooder, full of sweet talk and sympathy. The easiest way to find out is to ask a Pakistani friend what he thinks you should be doing. I Have.

Carl Murry, G-K Project
June 1963, Kushtia

I share this letter to help illustrate my naivety at that time and as a preface to a series of meetings in late July and early August that resulted in some significant changes.

The first meeting was an update by Mr. Ahmed on the progress made over the past year. It surprised me to learn that the number of acres irrigated was five times more than last year. Most of the canals were capable of delivering water. Farmers planted seven times more Aus, and yields per bigha had increased considerably. Special programs (such as the chicken vaccination service, tractor demonstration plots, monthly newsletter, seed multiplication project, seed selection and line planting efforts, fertilizer and pest control, cinema program, and the starting of Chasi Club) were having a positive impact. They reinforced the director's decision to expand services to the lower areas.

The following joint meetings of EPWAPDA, FAO, and Peace Corps resulted in some new assignments and support. A second Jeep, three Honda 50 motorbikes, and a trailer will be provided for the expansion.

Some of the new assignments include:

- Terry to join Will and Walt at Amala Research.
- Ken to assist Mr. Haque and Mr. Adullah in extension office in Kushtia.
- Art to assist Special Operations Office in Bheramara.
- Pete to Kushtia to continue Farm Management program.
- Marvin and George to work on Seed Multiplication and Poultry projects in addition to extension at Noapara.
- John and Ray to Irrigation Development Scheme and Extension in Bheramara.
- Harold to Water Quality and Surveying in Kushtia.
- Grant to Design Office in Kushtia.
- Carl to Chasi Club Development and Master Farmer program in Kushtia. ~And, I was officially assigned as Team Leader.

Pete harvested the Aus demonstration plot near Baradi, and it yielded 45 mds per acre, where the average yield is 8 to 10 mds/acre (one Maund equals about 82 lbs). The numbers impressed the farmers, but they acknowledged that the fertilizer was subsidized, and they couldn't afford to buy it without official intervention. We paid R5.50 per sack; they would be charged R25.00 at the government rate. The Boro Rice demonstration plot had shown a 600% increase, with stands reaching over five feet tall.

While awaiting the Hondas, Pete and I rode our bikes down to several villages in the lower canal areas, where they were not as familiar with the sight of foreigners. As we rode along the canal banks, we noticed that small groups of women would wade along the edge to do their laundry and take baths. On occasion, they would be completely nude, and rather than duck down in the water or try to cover themselves; they would simply cover their faces with their hands.

There was one village where the boys who tended the cattle would throw their tending sticks at the spokes of our bikes and call us "Red Monkeys." If the sticks went through the spokes, they caught on the wheel supports, which resulted in a very abrupt stop with damage to the spokes and the rider. The boys were usually around eight years old and ran away when we stopped. We would follow them on our bikes or on foot to their homes to explain to their parents that their behavior was not acceptable, and it seemed to work.

CHAPTER 26

A Letter Home

My mother kept most of the letters I wrote home, and I have been using them to help me recall the events that I am writing about. I have decided to share one of those letters.

August 5, 1963

Dear folks and family,

Sorry for the delay in answering your last letter. We received the package with the song books, agricultural slides from the Stevensons, and my replacement social security card and driver's license. Thank you for going to all that trouble.

Peaches must be in full swing with the Elbertas ready for picking. I know you all are putting in long hard hours!

We got the house cleaned up after our return from Kashmir and the smell is much better. Workmen are putting in electric wire for the fans and lights. They may have it finished by the time we leave. There are still piles of dirt, bricks and bamboo all over the yard and we have screens in the little kitchen.

Yesterday, we went to the Anglo-Saxon church here in Kushtia. There are only 6 members and two were absent. The complete service is in Bengali and there are a lot of words we don't know and it was kinda hard to follow but we enjoyed supporting them. They said we could hold a service in English when the boy's were in town. After church we went to the movie and saw "Siege of Sydney Street". It was raining so hard on the tin roof we couldn't hear a word. It has been raining 2 or 3 times a day.

Seems to be a lot of snake charmers around and those Cobras really give me the willies. The bats are active now. Every evening around 6 pm you might see 20 or 30 at one time. They are big, I bet some of them have a wing span of over four feet. I have seen a couple of giant lizards two to three feet long in addition to our tik tikies and geckos. With all the weird cloud formations, we have seen some really beautiful sunsets. Everything is so green and lush and beautiful. Still have prickly heat.

Paul Slawson is staying with us for a couple of days as we are having some reorganizational meetings this week that feel promising.

Tell Kenny that I am sorry to hear about his car, but he should have got a Ford. Tell Peggy to take good care of that little "Pot Belly" and we are excited for her and tell Donnie to not grind too many gears for Guli.

Love to you all, Carl and Carol [sic]

Other excerpts from other letters this month:

- *Soccer season is going full tilt here even in all this rain. Wednesday, August 14 is Pakistan Independence day and Carols students performed at a big school function in the morning. After lunch we went to Ujangram village for sports events and a disguise contest. I think the winner was a nude man who had tarred and feathered himself almost completely. Marvin Horst awed the crowd with his baton twirling performance. We topped off the day watching boat racing and a soccer game.*
- *On Saturday, August 24, 10 lady volunteers were able to visit Bheramara for a square dance party of three squares. Mr. and Mrs. Alexander hosted the event. He is a caller and brought some records with him. Two of the ladies who attended ended up marrying G-K men. (Art and Joanie and Walt and Jean).*
- *Boils are a pain in the butt! I had a couple earlier in the month that made riding a bicycle very uncomfortable. On the 28th a couple of them got so bad I could not sit down. Barbara lanced a couple of them, one of them twice, which was very painful and inspired me to try any alternatives suggested including hot water soaks. Boils and prickly heat are to be avoided.*
- *It must be breeding season for the Jackals because they sure have been doing a lot of howling and the bugs are driving us nuts. Harold and I have been trying to repair a canal for 3 days in order to save about R15,000 worth of rice. Today was a Bengali holiday so Carol and Barbara helped us try to plug gopher holes and were muddy.*

CHAPTER 27

Onward

The changes in our job descriptions helped define our roles and narrow our scope of activities. My responsibilities included:

1. Chasi Clubs
2. Master Farmer program
3. G-K Newsletter
4. Cinema Program
5. Team Leader

The Chasi (farmer) Clubs evolved from the irrigation committees and met once a month to learn topical agriculture practices, share experiences, and coordinate activities. Meeting with overseers once a month, we would prepare and practice a lesson plan with teaching aids to be used at our meetings. We established ten clubs:

1. Swastipur
2. Shalgharmandhua
3. Unjangram
4. Kirthi Nagar

5. Poshim Abdulpur
6. Noapara
7. Hazarati
8. Mashon
9. Barchada
10. Gopalpur

I attended each of the meetings, assisted in the presentation, gave a short talk, presented the cinema program, and participated in discussions. The Chief Extension Officer requested ten more clubs in the lower project as transportation became available.

The Master Farmer program provides a means of recognizing and rewarding those farmers who attend meetings, provide leadership, demonstrate good farming practices, and assist their communities.

Recognition may include a certificate, cash awards, trips to other projects, etc. Chasi Clubs develop the criteria.

Carl reviewing a monthly lesson with some overseers to be presented at Chasi Clubs in their areas.

We published the first issue of the G-K Newsletter in April 1963. It seemed to be very helpful and has received outstanding support from the overseers. It will continue to be published each month.

The Cinema program began as a result of our visit to USIS office in Dacca in December 1962 when they informed us that we could check out projectors, screens, generators, and films to show at our irrigation committee meetings. The number of agricultural and Bengali language films was very limited, so we would supplement them with general interest films such as Wilma Rudolf and Jesse Owens's Olympic performances, travel, and science films.

The Chasi Clubs not accessible by Jeep made arrangements to meet us with a bullock cart to carry the equipment. Crowds would come out to meet us, and kids yelled, "the ghosts are coming." We quickly learned to grab the screen and head for an open area to set it up. As the crowd jockeyed for viewing positions, we would have room to set up the generator and projector. Many of the villagers, especially in the lower project, had never seen motion pictures and were truly awed.

As the team leader, I was responsible for signing off on a myriad of chits – memos, orders, receipts, and notes of record that were a part of a very elaborate record-keeping process. The Peace Corps required me to communicate, coordinate, report, and liaison with the administration and our G-K Volunteers. An example of such records is as follows:

No. 1663/F-5 Dated. 6.5.63
To: The Asstt. Extension Officer, Kushtia
Subject: - Monthly report on the working of the pump

No. 21550 and No. 21679.
Ref: - His memo. No002 dated 26.4.63

The Team Leader of the Peace Corps Volunteers may be requested to send a report every month to you at its close showing the places of work, number of days of work, total hours of work, and area irrigated chasi club wise.

sd/
Extension Officer, EPWAPDA, Kushtia.

Memo. No. 1107 dt. 83
Copy to Team Leader for information and necessary action

One notice in August from the Peace Corps, Dacca asked for three volunteers to travel to Karachi and drive three Jeeps back across India to Dacca. Something had damaged the port in Chittagong, and we could not offload the Jeeps there. This sounded like a great adventure, and Art Sipma volunteered to be one of the drivers.

Mid-September, the Honda's arrived in Dacca, and Carol and I accompanied their shipment to Kushtia via the steamer. While we were there, we had our annual physical and chest x-rays. We were also able to make travel arrangements for our vacation to Thailand.

The Honda 50's were wonderful. Based in Bheramara and Kushtia, they were scheduled on request. As we expanded to the lower project, they were practically essential. One disadvantage we noted was they were not as versatile as the bicycles. We could ride bikes on very narrow paths, on field berms, small ditch banks, and carry them across shallow waterways and bamboo bridges. The Honda's weighed about 150 pounds and required a boat to ferry us across or some help in carrying them. Over several days, I logged over 70 miles on one.

In late September, it was still hot and muggy, but the rains eased up. We usually stay up until after midnight because it's too hot to sleep, and we often listen to "Voice of America" on our shortwave radio from 10:30 pm to 12:00 am. They were featuring Dave Brubeck and Crew and played "Take Five" just before the news. It was a real relief to hear President Kennedy declare that they were no longer drafting married men, so my deferment may not end in June unless the draft board decides that I have already been drafted, and my service has just been postponed. After these two years, I am not looking forward to serving two more back to back.

Now that the rains are easing up, we have tried to see a couple of English movies at the cinema on Sunday afternoons. There have been a couple of "Spaghetti" westerns and our favorite, "Three Stooges."

CHAPTER 28

Thailand

Our vacation to Thailand began on Saturday morning, October 12, at 3:00 am on a train ride to Calcutta. Since we originated our trip from Dacca, Air France provided a nice hotel on Saturday night, and our flight departed at 6:30 Sunday morning. Air France delayed our flight at our stop in Rangoon, Burma. We did not know why the delay was, but they bussed us into town with an escort of military jeeps with armed soldiers. The hotel served tea and instructed us not to leave the lobby area as the soldiers stood guard over us. After a couple of hours, we returned to the airport and continued our flight to Bangkok, arriving in the early afternoon.

The Peace Corps Offices were our first stop. I had developed sharp stomach pains and wanted to check with the Peace Corps Doctor. He could not diagnose the problem, but I was later diagnosed with a duodenal ulcer, which was the probable cause.

We stayed at the Peace Corps Hostel and visited with volunteers who had many good suggestions for us. On Monday and Tuesday, we looked around Bangkok and enjoyed eating American and Thai food, bowling, dancing, movies, loafing, and visiting with volunteers.

Wednesday morning, we participated in a rare event. The Queen of the Netherlands and her husband were visiting, and the King and Queen of Thailand hosted them in a very lavish Royal ceremony. The royalty took the Royal Barges on the Chao Phya River, which we observed.

In the afternoon, we boarded our train to travel down the Malayan Peninsula to the Freeport of Penang. It was a 28-hour trip in second class seats. The views were stunning, with plenty of wildlife, including working elephants, crocodiles, monkeys, giant lizards, birds, and other exotic scenes.

We arrived in Penang at about 8:00 pm on Thursday and were able to find a nice, comfortable hotel for $4.00. We spent most of Friday shopping for clothes, shoes, toiletries, and an excellent camera. A Zeiss Ikon with regular, wide-angle, and telescopic lenses was more than we needed. Saturday morning, we hired a mini-taxi to sightsee around Penang and then take us to Haad Yai to catch the 2:30 train up to Hua Hin. The driver had to stop for some personal business for about an hour but assured us that we had plenty of time. The train was gone when we pulled into town. However, what felt like a catastrophe turned into a delightful experience.

Songkla is a seaside resort about 25 miles from Haad Yai. The bus cost 10 cents apiece, and a beautiful room with a sliding glass door facing the beach cost $4.50. The new hotel was plush with TV, dancing, restaurants, spa, swimming pool, and many other amenities.

To make sure we didn't miss the train again, we took an early bus back to the train station. We had spent the last of our Baht at the hotel, and they were unable to cash traveler's checks. To our surprise, the train station also would not take traveler's checks, and being Sunday, all the banks were closed. Frantically, we searched for any business that would cash them. Finally, someone suggested we try the doctor's office, which was closed, of course. However, the doctor was at the office. He had received his medical training in the USA, was familiar with our problem, and cashed one for us.

Running to the train station, we just made our 2:30 departure time and had the luxury of just sitting quietly until the train departed at 2:45 pm. The next morning, just before we arrived at Hua Hin, we decided not to get off and went on to Bangkok.

After a shower at the Peace Corps Hostel, we went out for Pizza, shopped, made travel arrangements to return to Calcutta, and bought bus tickets for Pattaya. I ordered a tailor-made suit for $25, and Carol had her hair done. That night, we went to the Ambassador Club at the Erawan Hotel and enjoyed a beautiful show of Thai Classical dancing.

Pattaya is a small beach resort about 100 miles East of Bangkok and was a highlight of our trip. The bus dropped us off at a dirt road with a wooden sign that pointed toward the gulf and indicated Pattaya was 3 km. There were no vehicles on the road as we walked to the resort. We turned left to a thatched building on a bamboo pier that turned out to be the office, restaurant, rental shop, and cultural center. We rented a small bungalow with a thatched roof for three nights and went swimming in the beautiful, clear water.

That evening, we enjoyed a great seafood dinner and met a guy from Palo Alto, teaching English in Bangkok. He was traveling around the world crewing on tramp steamers.

He had worked for six weeks and would be moving on in two weeks. We visited and swapped stories for over an hour.

The next morning, we met him on the beach. He had rented a scuba outfit for the day and offered us a try at it. It was a humorous adventure as we rolled around in the surf with weighted belts, tanks, and flippers. After we got the hang of it, we discovered the absolute beauty of the reef and the abundance of sea life and decided to rent our own gear for the afternoon.

Thursday, we were swimming and snorkeling when a family from Bangkok beached their ski boat next to us for a lunch break. Since there were only four of them, they invited us to join them, and we shared the job of spotting. I loved skiing over the swells. We both learned to ski on one ski.

Later that afternoon, Carol had to return to the bungalow for something and soon returned breathlessly. She explained that there was a huge black snake in our bathroom. We found the manager and followed him to the room. He had a little stick about two-feet long that I expected him to use to kill the snake. He gently stroked it, rested the stick just behind its head, reached over and grasped it behind the head, and with a big smile, told us he would find another home for it. The snake was really harmless, he said. I have a long way to go to be able to handle snakes like that.

After another fabulous seafood dinner, we played pool and listened to a funky little band play Elvis Presley songs. Friday morning, we went for a final swim, packed up, and began our walk to the highway to catch the bus to Bangkok. This time, we caught a ride in a little, beat out, old Datsun pick-up. We arrived at the Peace Corps Hostel in time to clean up and go out to enjoy a movie.

On Saturday, we took a tour of the King's Palace, Marble Temple, and Wat Po. In the afternoon, we picked up my suit and did some shopping. We particularly enjoyed the weekend market in the park with kite fights and exotic goods.

Sunday was our last day in Thailand. We toured the Emerald Buddha site and other temples in the area before returning to the Sunday market for browsing and learning. In the late afternoon, we visited Alexander's son-in-law and family, went to the Feathers for dinner, and received an update on the G-K project.

Our return flight was on JAL and left Bangkok at 9:00 pm and arrived in Calcutta at 2 am. We slept late that morning at the Salvation Army Hostel. After some shopping, we caught the afternoon train and arrived in Kushtia at 2:45 am on Tuesday morning.

The visit to Thailand had a profound impact on me. I was overwhelmed by the kindness, graciousness, and joy of living in the Thai people. The children, at first, appeared similar to those in East Pakistan. They wore minimal clothing and lived in shacks or thatched huts, but their demeanor was much different. The Thai children seemed so happy. They played games, laughed, teased, sang songs, and sat quietly and respectfully when expected to do so. The pairing of young children and grandparents warmed my heart.

Material wealth did not seem so important, but the feelings of others were. Enough is good enough. Search for opportunities to give and help someone. Thais have a saying: "Mai Pen Lai," which means, "never mind." There was a book written of that title, and it is a good reflection of their attitude toward each other. Don't be worried, angry, or sad; instead, be happy and do something good.

Six years later, I returned to Thailand to work on a World Bank Project to improve Vocational Agriculture. Employed by Cal-Poly as part of a five-man team, we worked in cooperation with The Ministry of Education and the US State Department A.I.D. program. I lived and worked there for three years and still feel the need for a "Thai Fix" on occasion.

CHAPTER 29

Cooling

November and December bring less rain and cools down in the evenings. It feels invigorating, and I am inspired to work hard. My duties have settled into a manageable routine, and I am enjoying my work with the overseers in the Chasi Clubs.

There seems to be a growing need for a reference center or library, and I have begun inquiries to the Ministry of Agriculture, FAO, USAID, and USIS in regard to materials that might be made available to us and G-K Kushtia for a possible site.

The cooling brings new concerns. After a physically demanding day, a cold shower is less appealing than it had been. Heating a little water for spit baths becomes a more popular choice and worth the bother.

The temperature often drops to around 40 degrees, and while that may not sound so bad, there is no indoor heating, which makes your blanket a best friend and a precious possession. In the mornings, you search out a spot to await and welcome the morning sun as you begin your work in a reptilian manner.

Our November highlight turned into a low point in our lives. The Alexanders hosted a Thanksgiving party in Bheramara, with square dancing on Saturday, November 23. A 19-hour poker game followed, which was interrupted by a rumor that the President had been shot. Most of us did not believe it. It must be a mistake in translation or something. None of us had our shortwave radios for BBC or VOA transmissions, and it was in the middle of the night. The next morning, the news confirmed the assassination. President Kennedy was dead – shot and killed in Dallas, Texas. STUNNED!

Slowly, the details filtered in and coupled with all the reports of African-Americans being attacked with clubs, vicious dogs, and water cannons in the South caused a great deal of concern for what was happening in our country.

The Alexanders completed their assignment with FAO and returned home to Washington State on December 8. They were kind and helpful to all of us, and we will miss them very much.

Mr. W. Blackie was the FAO Team leader and filled in for Mr. Alexander after his departure. He was from New Zealand and shared some of his pictures and experiences with us. I was impressed with its natural resources, fishing, agriculture, and beauty and decided that I would try to visit there someday.

Sugar Cane planting is underway, and some Aman and Boro rice has matured. We have started conducting crop cuttings. One morning, Pete and I were taking a cutting, and we heard the Jeep horn honking. We had parked the Jeep on a canal bank about 200 yards away. Thinking that some kids were fooling around, we went to check it out and found a farmer struggling in the driver's seat. His eyes were the size of silver dollars as he tried to scoot down, in obvious panic. He had fastened the seat belt and couldn't figure out how to undo it.

Our neighborhood convenience store was a small, elevated structure about four by six feet, built similar to a rabbit hutch, with a drop-down door that could serve as an awning when propped up. The old man sat on a cushion surrounded by his goods, which included – pan leaf, betel nut, King Stork cigarettes, eggs, rice, bananas, peanuts, matches, crackers, and a variety of other essentials. One morning, I noticed a familiar object. My parents had gone to see a movie, "How the West Was Won," and sent us a postcard, which was now for sale in his little shop.

Our local convenience store located near our house came in Handy at times.

The letter writers are delightful. Many people are illiterate or are not fluent enough in another language to write a letter. So, you may find a writer hanging around the post office, or the postmaster may be able to refer you to one. Letter writers will translate and write out the letter for you. Some are multilingual, while others may specialize in French, Chinese, Arabic, Sanskrit, or other languages. Their skill levels and styles vary from formal English to their "best-effort" in a really foreign language. A delightful example of a letter received is as follows:

Santinagar
412

Dear Mr. Carl,

My best compliments to you and your Mrs. At first take my love and I hope you are quite well by the bless of God.

Those days when we altogether went to Amala and other place, your sweet uttering made me charmed and got me slightly into your customs.

I remember off and on and tell about you to my friends and show to them the book you presented me.

Wishing a happy and successful hours at Pakistani soil, let me say goodbye. Thank you.

Yours ever,
Kahlil [*sic*]

There have been several reports of Cholera outbreaks around the end of November. It seems to be more prevalent during this time of the year.

The Peace Corps is hosting a conference at Cox's Bazar over Christmas, and we plan to leave via the Steamer on December 21.

CHAPTER 30

Cox's Bazar

Christmas is a great time for a conference as it provides an opportunity for volunteers to share and support each other as a family during an important holiday. We departed Kushtia by train Saturday afternoon, December 21, and took the overnight steamer to Dacca. On Sunday, we flew to Chittagong and took a bus to Cox's Bazar. Our beach-side conference center exceeded our expectations for comfort and ambiance.

The schedule allowed for a lot of free time in the afternoons and evenings. Christmas was a free day. Swimming, surfing, and touch football games in the sand were popular in the afternoons, and music, dancing, card games, and visiting were enjoyed in the evenings. On Christmas Eve, we joined together to sing carols.

Several of us walked down to the wharf. Boats unloaded their catches for the day, and the variety and amount of fish they were catching amazed us. We saw swordfish, sharks, stingrays, and many unknown smaller fish. We asked a fisherman about the swordfish, and he said it was the right season for them and fishing was good now. As we walked back, a fisherman stopped us and asked if we would like to go fishing tomorrow. He pointed to a boat about 25-feet long with a big sail. Pete, Terry, and I decided ten rupees each was reasonable and agreed to meet him here at 5:30 am. Since it was Christmas morning, I would be up early anyway to see what Santa brought for me.

Up at five and on the beach at 5:30 am, we watched the boats load up and push out to sea. We waited and waited until he finally showed up at 7 am with three bamboo poles with a hank of string, small hooks, and sinkers. His boat turned out to be a 12-foot dugout, with a set of oars and a push pole. Even after lowering our expectations, this did not look like it would end well, and we terminated our contract. Dejected, we trudged back to the center, with visions of Swordfish dancing on the end of our lines. We stumbled across the carcass of a five-foot hammerhead shark and considered carrying it triumphantly back for all to see, but the smell wasn't worth it.

At the time, it did not seem like a Christmas to remember, but it was!

Returning to Kushtia on Saturday the 28th, I felt the pressure of getting the newsletter out, making monthly reports, and preparing for a ten-day training program for new overseers at Baradi Training Center starting January 6.

New Year's Eve featured goodies brought from Dacca, some beer and hard liquor, a short-wave sputtering and popping account of a football game (I think Texas beat Navy 28-6), and, of course, a marathon poker game.

Early January, communal riots began in Kashmir when someone stole hair from the Prophet. The Muslims accused the Hindus of the theft. Riots have been rippling across the subcontinent through New Delhi, Calcutta, and now into

Dacca and Bengal. Basically, the Hindus of India would expel Muslim families from their homes and deport them to Pakistan, and the Muslims of Pakistan would expel Hindus and deport them to India. In the process, there was much fighting, burning, killing, and destruction.

Opportunists used the conflict to steal and destroy. The trains have been frequent targets. The robbers pull the train's emergency stops, rob, and sometimes kill passengers, and they escape on prearranged transport. The Peace Corps sent a telegram asking volunteers not to travel until further notice.

The disruption has stopped mail delivery, food, supplies, caused curfews and created a general feeling of unease. The District Commissioner and a military official flew in by Helicopter and landed in a field across the road about 50 yards from our house. The pilot came over to our house and had tea while the D. was speaking on preventing violence.

I picked up another bug for about three days, with high fever and flu-like symptoms. I got better before starting any meds.

Ramadan starts on Thursday, January 16, and things will slow down for a while.

CHAPTER 31

Shame On Me

Losing your temper is embarrassing to those witnessing it, especially in Asian cultures. It might be compared to wetting your pants in front of everyone. In my family, it was an expected and frequent expression of anger when things deviated from expectations. My family expressed tempers verbally and often with the physical acts of throwing, hitting, kicking, and other 'relieving' actions, depending on severity. I work hard at controlling my temper.

On January 2, I received notice that our long-awaited trailer had arrived at the Kushtia train station. I notified the extension officer and requested that they send a truck to the station to pick it up. He suggested that I send a memo to the motor pool, which I did.

The training session for our new bunch of overseers started on January 6 and was extremely time-consuming. On the 8th, I was sick with a high temperature and flu-like symptoms for three days. On the 14th, I went to the motor pool to ask why the trailer had not been picked up, as we had an urgent need for it. They told me that the driver had gone to his village for the weekend and had not returned yet but would be there soon. When I returned on the 17th, the office was closed. Ramadan had started on the 16th, the day before, and many workers were absent today.

On the 20th, they informed me that the driver was ill and had not returned. There was a flatbed truck sitting in the yard, and I asked if I could use it. I showed him my Bengal driver's license and my class-A truck driving license and explained that I had much experience driving trucks. He said they would find another driver from Bheramara and pick it up soon. The truck was still sitting there on the 23rd, and I was told that the driver had taken the keys with him, but they would try to get them. I offered to hotwire the truck to start it. Of course, he could not give permission for me to do so.

On the 27th, I informed him that I had a meeting in Gopalpur that afternoon, but I would pick up the truck Wednesday the 29th. Nervous and with some apprehension, I jumped the ignition at 9 am on the 29th, and drove to the railway station. They had locked up the storage depot, and the person in charge told me that I needed to bring a permit from the station master before he could open up. The station master was talking with someone, so I had to wait. After 30 or 40 minutes, I knocked, opened the door, and apologized for the interruption. I asked for a note to release the trailer. My interruption must have irritated him. "Yes, Yes, just wait a moment," he replied.

Fifteen minutes later, he invited me in to have a seat. I declined to sit. "All I need is a note to release the trailer," I said. He asked if I had the documents. I explained that I had given them to the WAPDA motor pool, but the notice had come from this office on January 2, and surely there was a record of it in the logs. He called for an assistant and left the room. After what seemed like an eternity, he returned with a book and said the trailer had arrived on December 10 and that there may be some storage costs to clear up. I reminded him that we did not get a notice until January 2, but WAPDA would pay for them if there were charges.

Finally, he gave me a permit. I hurried back to the storage depot only to learn that it was past noon, and the person with the key was gone for his lunch break, even though it was Ramadan. Thankfully, he returned after an hour and fifteen minutes, and we found the trailer, which consisted of an axle, two wheels, and a wooden box about six-feet by eight-feet.

I asked if I could hire a chokie (porter) to help me. He said I needed to pay R25.00 for four men to help me. I laughed and said I only needed one or two, and R1.00 per person would be very generous. "No Sahib, these men are sanctioned by the railway, and others cannot come in," he said. They all laughed like they had me over a barrel, and I lost control. I told them to go to hell (Ja hanamay jao); I will do it myself.

The axle weighed about 130 pounds and wasn't very difficult to carry; the wheels were about 30 pounds each and were easy. The box, however, weighed over 300 pounds and was incredibly awkward to move on my own. I would tip it up on end and let it fall forward, clear the path, and tip it again. It made a lot of noise, and a crowd gathered around me as I rolled it out. At one point, I had to turn it on edge to get between some sacks of rice, and the box ripped the side of one sack as it fell. I managed to move the box to the bed of the truck, so all I had to do was slide it on, but I was having trouble lifting it. Finally, two of the chokies stepped in and helped me slide it on. I gave them each a rupee, went back and cleaned up the rice, jumped the ignition on the truck, and drove back to the compound.

After unloading the trailer at our house, I returned the truck to the yard, removed my pins, and walked home. The possible consequences of my actions began to grow, and I felt ashamed and worried, expecting the police to arrive at any time. My actions were definitely not an accepted Peace Corps practice, and I didn't tell anyone except Carol and Barbara. Our hosts must have written it off as a pagol (crazy) American thing because I never heard anything else about it.

The riots continued through most of January but have become sporadic now. They have caused a lot of disruption in transportation and communication throughout the country. Ten new Chasi Clubs will soon be added to our program, and I have spent much time in the lower project.

The Asia Foundation has donated thirty new books to our Library, but we are still searching for a room to use.

The kerosene refrigerator needs repair, and Jesore needs some medical supplies, so Peace Corps asked me to drive to Khulna, which is at the northern edge of the Sundarbans.

CHAPTER 32

Sundarbans

The Sundarbans are a huge mangrove forest located on the vast mudflats formed by the confluence of five or more major rivers, including the Ganges. The delta floods during the rainy season and is subject to the tides, which dictate times of travel. It is home to the Royal Bengal Tigers and a wide variety of birds and animals.

Five of us decided to extend our trip to Khulna and visit the Sundarbans. Carol, Ken, Pete, Grant, and I dropped the refrigerator off on Wednesday afternoon after a long day's drive that included several "homemade" ferry crossings. We found rooms at a rest house, and the next morning we caught a service launch to Mongla Port. The launch was like a local bus service that makes stops frequently along the river. It costs .40 cents each and took about six hours to complete.

Not realizing the trip would be so long, we did not bring any food or water. It was Ramadan, so none was available on the boat or at any of the stops. It made the trip feel much longer.

Two Italian Catholic Fathers were returning to Mongla

Port after visiting students to let them know it was safe to return to school. They had adjourned because of the riots. We had noticed some of the village houses had white crosses painted on them. The Fathers explained that the families wanted the rioters to know they were Christians and not Hindus.

Visiting with them was interesting. They could not speak English, so we had to converse in Bengali. We asked if they knew the location of the rest house, and they informed us that there was no rest house, but we were welcome to stay with them at the mission school. Students would not return until after Eid holidays. How fortunate for us.

They provided us with beds, and the cooks had a huge pot of stew and home-baked bread (without flies) waiting for us. We were famished and truly felt blessed and thankful for these men. One of the cooks had a relative who had a boat and was willing to take us into the forests.

You must plan boat travel around the tides, and we were fortunate that the high tide on Friday was at 1:00 pm. The boat was a wooden dugout, about 12-feet long for the six of us. The boatman had a pole and three paddles. It was wide enough that two could sit side by side and take turns paddling. We took the low tide at 7:00 am and were able to be out on the bay before the current picked up.

There were about ten freighters anchored in the bay, offloading onto smaller ships. We had to paddle alongside a Russian freighter for a while, and crewmen shouted, waved, and offered us vodka. It was absolutely eerie paddling out into the enormous bay in a little leaky boat with three inches of freeboard in large swells.

On the other side of the bay, we entered a wide channel. The tide carried us along faster than we could paddle. The channel narrowed, and the water-level lifted us to where we could see the flora and fauna. We soon arrived at a woodcutter's home built on a raised platform with a small dock.

After a short visit with the woodcutter, he guided us to a trail leading into the forest, cautioning us that the tide was still rising and the trail would soon be underwater in places. We should return before 1:00 pm. The trail was difficult, with many knobs sticking up from the roots. The path led to an open area, where men had cut wood and grew patches of boro rice. With soggy shoes and scratched up legs, we hurried back without seeing any Tigers.

Joining other boats, we rode the receding tide out to the bay and endured the long paddle across to Mongla Port. We cut palm leaves to use as shade. The Catholic School was not far from the docks, so we were able to purchase some gifts for the school and the cooks before leaving the next morning.

Saturday, Feb. 15, was Eid, the end of Ramadan, and the trip on the boat back to Khulna was one big party. We feasted on free food and goodies. We picked up the refrigerator, spent the night in Khulna, and attended several parties before returning to Kushtia on Sunday the 16th.

Several river crossings were made by lashing two boats together and installing wooden planks to carry the Jeep across.

The little boat the cook arranged for us to travel across the Bay and into the Sunderbans. Clockwise from the front Grant Wells, Ken Jaeger, Carol, boatman and Carl. Photo taken by Pete Hansen.

Scene along the riverside near Mongla Port.

An amazing sight of an elephant being transported on the river.

CHAPTER 33

Foreboding News

As the Eid Holidays came to an end, the work schedule began to return to normal. We made up many postponed meetings and brought back the cinema program. We set aside a room for our library, and various sources sent books.

Peace Corps set June 7th as our termination date, and we began to make plans for our extended trip home via Europe. I made an application to Cal-Poly to continue my teacher training program in the fall of 1964.

A letter from Carol's dad informed us that her mother, Francis, was not feeling well and needed surgery. However, he told us not to worry because they didn't want it to interfere with our service in Pakistan. We worried anyway.

The beard I started growing in December is finally starting to look good. My friends call me "Boro Bhai," Big Brother, as most of them wear beards.

New Chasi Clubs in the lower project have been started and include:

- Shalodag
- T1K

- Poradaha
- Kharara
- Osmanpur
- Khazanager
- Ballarpur
- Kirthinager
- Jagannathpur

It is a unique feeling working in the lower project as many young people have never seen Europeans or any movies, so we are the center of attraction in many cases. A common practice is feeling the hair on our forearms.

We will have six days of vacation left, so we decided to take a trip to Delhi, Agra, and Darjeeling in early April.

Hossain Ahmed, Overseer from Gopalpur, has asked me to accompany him to his bridal negotiations in early March.

CHAPTER 34

The Marriage

"So, Mr. 'Cahl' Sahib, would you join me, my brother, and my uncle for my proposal meeting at the home of the woman who has been selected to be my wife?"

"Well, I guess so, Hossain, but why would you choose me to come?" I asked.

"You are my friend and can help explain to my future father-in-law why it is important to my future employment that I be provided with a Honda motor bike. This is the meeting where we set the terms of our marriage contract. I am pleased with the woman who has been selected, and I know her father could afford to buy me one."

"I thought that the man paid the dowry?"

"There are many terms in the contract that I will propose, and, of course, I will provide gifts to her family to insure her confidence and security."

"Have you met her?"

"I know of her family, and may have seen her from some distance, but we have never actually met. She is 14 years old now and must keep purdah. In your country, I have heard that you practice love-marriage, is that true?"

"Yes," I replied. "It is hard for us to imagine marrying someone without dating and getting to know them well before deciding to marry, and we want it to be our decision and not our parents'."

"But physical attraction to each other may blind a person's consideration of other very important factors that are basic to a good marriage, such as faith, customs, family compatibility, goals, and standards of behavior. We trust that our parents love us and will want to choose the best for us."

"It seems that you enter into marriage with low expectations and try to make the best of it and then learn to love and appreciate each other and build relationships so that the marriage seems to get better and feels successful. While we enter into marriage with high expectations and dreams of happiness that are very difficult to achieve and often become disappointed," I generalized.

"The part that we have in common is that marriage requires commitment to be successful. Can you pick me up on your Honda at Gopalpur Chasi Club around 7 pm?" Hossain asked.

It was becoming dark. We met Hossain's brother at the entrance to the compound, and the bride's family escorted us to an enclosed dining area that was elevated off the ground level and covered with thatch. There was a large table about 18 inches tall with mats and some cushions to sit on.

An old man played sitar in the yard outside the meeting area. A young man with small drums and another with a flute accompanied him. Children ran around in the yard playing, but not a single woman was present.

Eight of us sat around the table, and we made

introductions. The family served tea and a variety of snacks. In the beginning, we visited, talking slowly and clearly so that I could participate. They asked about my family, and Hossain asked me many questions about how valuable the Honda was to my work, and how it could help him advance in his profession. Then, there were the standard questions of why is the United States using clubs and dogs to suppress peaceful black citizens, why is the USA government giving arms and aid to India, and why did Marilyn Monroe commit suicide? Who killed John F. Kennedy?

About 9 pm, the hosts brought a large bowl of biryani, with pieces of roasted goat, soup, and lentils, for us to eat. As the meal finished, the conversation's tempo and vocabulary increased to the point where it was difficult for me to keep up, and the negotiations became obvious. Sometime after midnight, I dozed off and didn't wake up until it was breaking dawn.

Hossain was smiling as he explained that his proposal had been accepted around 3 am, and the family had invited us to spend the rest of the night and join them for breakfast before returning.

They held the wedding ceremony about a month later in Kushtia, and Carol and I attended. It was a big party. The bride sat in the lotus position on a big cushion. Elaborately dressed, she wore a lot of makeup and of henna markings. Her attendants scurried around, making adjustments, alterations, and primping her in a teasing manner with lots of laughter.

The space grew quiet as Hossain entered the room from behind, and without making eye contact with anyone, he sat on a cushion to her right, looking straight forward. The noise began to build again as the girls tried to cajole the bride into looking at him. They used mirrors and many different tricks. Gradually, the whole crowd involved themselves in trying to get them to look at each other.

Finally, they joined hands, peeking at each other with much blushing and grinning. An official of Islam then conducted the ceremony with an overview of the contract. The party continued as we left in the wee hours.

The entire process follows instructions from the Quran. Men may marry up to four wives, with the stipulation that he must treat the women equally.

A man may divorce a wife by going to her on the full moon and telling her, "I hereby divorce you." He must then repeat this process for three full moons in a row. Of course, he must return her dowry as well.

It was special to me to be a part of this ceremony, and I will always appreciate the memories and experience.

CHAPTER 35

Marching On

The Month of March was hectic and productive. In addition to the 26 Chasi Club meetings, I taught 40 hours at Baradi Training Center, officially opened the library, continued the cinema program, and published the G-K Extension News.

Plans for our trip home were coming together as we researched routes, contacts, dates, and costs. Leaving Dacca on June 7, we would fly to Delhi and visit Agra, Tehran, Beirut, Istanbul, Athens, and Naples. From Naples, we take a train to Munich, Germany, buy a Volkswagen, and drive around Europe using the book "Europe on $5 a Day" as a guide. We end up in Lisbon, Portugal, around August 15, ship the VW home, and fly home via New York.

We modified the trip from April 17 to 23 to just include – Calcutta to Patna and the little blue train to Darjeeling and Bhutan.

Carol was having some difficult stomach problems, and we had to make a trip to Dacca to check them out. Shortly after her return, we received a letter from her dad, informing us that her mom's surgery did not go well and that she would have to remain in the hospital for further tests. Two days later, we received a telegram from Carol's Aunt Ruth, asking Carol to call her.

Ruth informed us that Francis, Carol's mom, had cancer and could not remove it. The cancer had spread. The doctors said that she probably had less than two months to live. She apologized for interfering because her mom did not want us to come home early but thought we should be informed and make our own decision. So glad she did!

The Peace Corps was very gracious and helpful and offered us two termination options. We could take a two-week personal leave and return to finish up our service, or we could terminate a month early. The advantage of the two-week leave is that we could leave immediately and be back to complete service activities, job transfers, and farewell parties and then return home.

Given the seriousness of Francis's condition, the decision was easy. We packed up, arranged for others to take over our duties, wrote reports and recommendations, and said our goodbyes to as many as possible.

On our last day in Kushtia, April 27, a large hurricane passed through. It rained and stormed most of the day, but just before 3 pm, the sky turned green and swirling black. The winds increased to 80 to 90 mph. We sat in the bedroom with our backs against the brick walls as the glass in the windows blew out and scattered across the room. The floor flooded with pools of water and a variety of debris. The sounds were deafening and made it very difficult to talk. After 40 to 45 minutes, the wind began to decrease, and it returned to the more normal storm.

On the 28th, we took the morning train to Faridpur with all of our luggage to catch the overnight steamer to Dacca.

The debris from the storm was extensive and caused many detours on the way to the station. There were minor delays on the train, but it was less than 2 hours late reaching the docks.

Reaching the Peace Corps offices shortly after lunch, we began our checking-out process, which included a brief medical exam and arrangements for a complete termination physical once we were home. I tipped the scales at 138 pounds, which amounted to a loss of 40 pounds. We turned in our sleeping roles and other items issued to us and left other things that volunteers might be able to use at the hostel.

April 30, 1964 was our official date of termination. I don't remember much about that day except that I was looking forward to a good meal on our SAS flight to Hong Kong. After all that we had been through in our final days, it is difficult to explain why I almost burst into tears when offered the choice of RICE and Curry or RICE and Chicken. Oh no, not Rice!

In Hong Kong, we transferred to a Pan Am flight and flew to San Francisco via Honolulu. We arrived home on Saturday, May 2, 1964.

Francis died on June 7, 1964, which was to be our last day of service.

EPILOGUE

CHAPTER 36

Good? Bad? Shrug?

How was it? Did you do any good? Would you do it again? My first response was, "Hard; I'm not sure; and No." I now know that it was truly an amazing experience that took time to appreciate, and its value to me has increased every day of my life.

Did the two years of Peace Corps service meet my expectations? I would have to answer "no." I expected to show locals how to increase their crop yields and physically do so. Instead, I discovered competent farmers capable of producing much more if given the resources and a model of how to organize and work cooperatively. I learned their ways and customs. I shared their frustrations and helplessness. I worked shoulder to shoulder with men, building a bond of understanding and friendship that could not be gained in any other way.

The true value of this experience is understanding and appreciation on both sides of the relationship. Locals can create an image of Americans beyond depictions in their newspapers of soldiers, racists, amoral Hollywood characters, and "ugly American tourists." We can share with our fellow Americans the culture, religious understanding, resources, needs, and the desire to be friends of our host nations.

There is an old saying about a man who felt sorry for himself because he had no shoes until he met a man with no feet. I often feel that way when I hear folks complaining about taxes, temporary loss of electricity, costs of commodities, and infringement of individual rights. I remember my days in Bangladesh.

Perhaps my biggest regret is my failure to share my experiences with those here at home. When I hear blanket condemnations of Muslims and generalizations of third world countries, I need to speak out.

The preface, "One Town World," presented a situation that we face every day in our communities, states, and countries of the world. I challenge you to come up with what you feel is the best solution.

I choose the strategy of providing and improving basic human needs and building bridges of communication for those in need. Distancing, building walls, pressuring, guarding and protecting our precious resources and stockpiles seem to be the choice of an increasing number of our citizens.

It is my opinion that most people want to live in the area of their family and ancestors. The comforts of customs, religion, and shared values are difficult to give up unless the basic human needs of food, shelter, health, and safety are threatened. How can we help make conditions better for them?

1. The Peace Corps has been the most effective foreign relations program in our history. Most people do

not realize the impact that it has had over the last 60 years – providing assistance, communicating, building bridges, and, maybe most importantly, our knowledge and awareness of the world community. In the chess game of life, do not underestimate the power of pawns.

2. The US State Department's AID program, which provides targeted funding and guidance to critical development projects.
3. Leadership of Congress and the President to identify and act upon violations of human rights globally basis and apply political pressure to rectify them.

In the process of recalling and writing my Peace Corps experiences, it surprised me at how naive and judgmental I was. There were times I felt racist and condescending in my eagerness to "Get'er Done." Looking back, I wish I had listened and learned for the first six months before I even offered a suggestion or word of advice.

My advice to prospective volunteers is to understand the job the host country is asking you to do and commit yourself to do it to the best of your ability. Develop a personal, secondary project that reflects your interests or special abilities to share with your community – such as music, gardening, sewing, cooking, sports, food preservation, woodworking, or whatever. Take advantage of every opportunity to participate in social activities. Savor and maintain the personal relationships that evolve.

The third goal of the Peace Corps is to help promote a better understanding of other peoples on the part of Americans. School presentations, community action groups, and personal relationships do not seem to be enough. I hope this written account will help further this goal.

One disadvantage of my choice to serve in the Peace Corps was that I forfeited the privilege of being a veteran with the honor and perks therein. In my day, every young man was drafted and processed. It was not a choice. I don't want to sound petty or disrespectful, but it does bother me that the Peace Corps does not receive the acknowledgement and respect for its service to our country. I feel strongly that every American should spend at least one year in service to the nation.

Since my Peace Corps service, I spent three years in Thailand working on a World Bank project to Improve Vocational Agriculture. I was Crops Advisor on a five-man team from Cal-Poly in partnership with US AID.

In Swaziland, I spent two and a half years as Associate Director for Agriculture, Education, and Appropriate Technologies for the Peace Corps.

In my domestic life, I worked as an Agriculture Teacher and School Counselor.

CHAPTER 37

First Conference

"Citizens in a Time of Change" was the theme on the invitation to attend the first national returned Peace Corps Volunteers conference in WashingtonD., March 5-7, 1965. We responded with regret because we could not afford the cost. Peace Corps offered us a travel grant and room and board with a volunteer host.

Our flight from Santa Maria connected with the "Red-Eye" from LAX, and we arrived at National Airport around 5:30 am Friday and took a shuttle to the Mall. Registration was in the beautiful, flag-lined lobby of the State Department Building, where we received packets, badges, and a very warm welcome. The conference listed host families on a bulletin board, and it delighted us to learn that Kingston Berlew, our Peace Corps Director in Pakistan, would be our host. We met some friends from West Pakistan and were visiting when staff invited us into a conference room for an interview with Newsweek Magazine, which seemed to go well.

The Berlews' paged us, and we met at the bulletin board. They drove us to their beautiful home on the Potomac

River, about ten miles away in Virginia. Bright red cardinals flitted around in the branches of dormant trees, covered in light snow, on the riverbanks. The warm fireplace emitted a glow of comfort as we began to nod off and were excused for a nap before the opening session.

The buffet dinner upstairs in the banquet hall was amazing. As we stepped out of the elevator, Sargent Shriver, a reception line of dignitaries, and sponsoring hosts greeted us. The elegance of decor and quality and quantity of food overwhelmed me. There were chandeliers, ice sculptures, mountains of strawberries, furniture, historical paintings, and works of art.

Two serving tables with lines on each side offered such a variety of food that I found myself engrossed in making selections. The man across the table asked in which country I served. I looked up to see a man I knew and gushed out, "East Pakistan, Sir., Vice President Humphrey, what an honor to meet you. One of our team members, Barbara Baden, is from Minnesota, and she really likes you!" We went on to talk about the G-K project. A guy behind me in line with a Texan accent joined in and sat near us to eat. He was very friendly and easy to talk to, and I later found out he was a journalist named Bill Moyer.

Some of the speakers in our opening session included Sargent Shriver, Vice President Hubert Humphrey, Secretary of State Dean Rusk, and Secretary of Defense Robert McNamara. While waiting for the elevator, we were standing next to a person Carol recognized right away, and they began to converse about his music during the ride down to the auditorium. Harry Belafonte sang "We Shall Overcome" in closing the session.

Participants included approximately 800 volunteers

and about 200 representatives from business, government, media, and private interests. There were 24 discussion groups in breakout rooms of about 45 each. I joined the group on primary and secondary education, and Carol participated in the international affairs group.

Saturday evening, Peace Corps held invitation-only receptions to ten homes in the area. Our invitation was at the Todd Lincoln home in Georgetown for cocktails and a buffet dinner. It was a beautiful home, and I enjoyed discussions with the Secretary of Health, Education, and Welfare, Anthony Celebreezze, Secretary of Commerce, Connor, Assistant Secretary of Labor, Daniel Moynihan, and Columnist Elmo Roper, who had some thought-provoking questions that I really appreciated.

A reunion of Pakistan volunteers at Dr. Goldstone's home followed the receptions and lasted until about 4 am.

Sunday's sessions were reports on the breakout sessions and attempts to arrive at some consensus on the role of returned Peace Corps Volunteers and what, if any, kind of organization we might form.

We had heated discussions regarding the purpose and function of such an organization. Most objected to being a political entity for influence. Instead, the majority favored of a service for sharing and networking our experiences to our communities.

As the conference was ending Sunday afternoon, Peace Corps asked me to meet with Sargent Shriver and some people from Southern University, Baton Rouge, LA. They asked if I could stay over an extra day and meet Monday for a proposed position in Africa. I agreed, and they arranged hotel accommodations and rescheduled our flight.

Sunday Evening, friends from East Pakistan, Walt and

Jean Winnant, gave us a tour of Washington DC and invited us to have dinner with them at their home in Maryland.

Congressman Burt Talcott and Senator Kuchel invited us to their offices for a TV interview and tour, but I was busy all day with my discussions with Southern University. Carol and our friend Barbara Baden went to Kuchel's office, and he gave them a permit to watch congress in-session and take a congressional tour of the White House.

Southern University was recruiting me to be the director of Peace Corps agricultural programs in five western, francophone countries in West Africa. I would be stationed in Conakry, Guinea, be responsible for identifying appropriate agricultural jobs, and help select, train, and supervise volunteers. It seemed to be a fit, and they wanted me to visit the campus on Wednesday. I had to refuse because of my commitments at school, and we made arrangements for a later date.

I took more interviews with the Peace Corps on Tuesday morning before our noon flight home. That weekend, March 14, I had the TV show, "Agriculture USA" in Burbank, and the following weekend, March 20, was Art and Joanie Sipmas wedding near Disneyland. Suddenly, it was time to visit Southern University and Washington DC again.

Just before I went, a notice appeared on the job opening board that the agricultural teaching position in Sonora, CA had opened up. This was my dream job, and I could not afford to apply. Carol agreed, so we postponed the trip until after the interview. I was chosen to be the agriculture teacher at Sonora Union High School.

CHAPTER 38

The Trip Home

Six years after the original plan, we had just completed a three-year assignment in Thailand and again planned our trip home through Europe. It would start with a return to East Pakistan and a visit to Kushtia with our three children, Sean (4), Kerry (2), and Heather (1).

After some delays, we arrived a little after 10 pm and took a bus to the once-famous Shabaugh Hotel, which had been beyond our means as Peace Corps Volunteers and had a distinctive high classed, British atmosphere about it. It had recently rained, and the streets were full of water, and with the heat and humidity, our memories were aroused.

The next morning we took two rickshaws to the nearest train station and boarded the train to Kushtia. Arriving at Poradaha Junction at 11:30 am, I was surprised at the absence of food wallas (vendors). Normally, there would be hawkers with bread, bananas, eggs, peanuts, rice, betel nut, cigarettes, tea, and other items to sell to passengers through the windows or on the platform. There was none, not even tea.

Waiting in a small, dirty room, surrounded by 50 or

60 well-wishers, we learned that the ten-minute train change would likely be longer as the schedules had been discontinued some months earlier. The train would arrive when it got there. The lack of food, trains off schedule, and the subdued atmosphere gave me an eerie feeling.

The train arrived four hours late, at 3:30 pm, and we arrived in Kushtia 20 minutes later. Taking rickshaws to the G-K Colony, we then waited an hour and a half for them to arrange two beds at the rest house. While waiting, we walked around the neighborhood, visiting our old house and familiar areas that had markedly declined in appearance and upkeep. We met several acquaintances and visited as much as possible while tending to our mistreated children.

The hostel served dinner at 8 pm. The rice and curry was too hot (spicy) for the kids, but I could get a bowl of plain rice for them. There were no biscuits, fruit, or custard with the meal, and tea was served for dessert.

The next morning, after toast and tea, I set out to cash a twenty-dollar traveler's check at the bank and check on the train to Ishurdi. The ordeal took an hour and a half, three cups of tea, and despite not having a written agreement with the US government, the manager took a personal risk and a 30% commission to advance me 70 Rupees. I actually felt grateful. The train from Faridpur had been cancelled.

Carol and the kids were visiting with friends when I returned. One of the friends suggested that we catch the 11:30 am Poradaha train at Bheramara, but we would have to hurry. I ran to town and hired a motorized rickshaw (Samlor). It has a small motorbike engine and a seat about 30 inches wide and 24 inches deep. Two people face forward, and two people face the rear. Eight of us and our bags piled on with the driver's assistant and our friend standing on the rear bumper.

The little engine did very well under the load, and we were making pretty good time when a tire blew out. The assistant and our friend took the tire and started walking back to Kushtia. We would certainly miss the train, but we might be able to catch the 1:30 ferry. An old truck came by and slowed for the group of us waiting. I jumped on the back and returned to Kushtia and hired another Samlor. Passing our friend and the assistant, I stopped and explained our plans and picked up our friend. I paid the first Samlor driver his full fare, and he was grateful as we headed off in a cloud of dust.

It was almost 1 pm as we approached the ferry, which appeared to be all loaded and ready to go. The little Samlor was going full speed with the engine screaming and the dust billowing around us as we yelled and waved our arms for them to wait for us.

No problem! The gangplank was down, and we drove straight on board and clambered to the deck, ready to take off. The passengers gathered around us, and we learned that the Captain was waiting now. Relief evolved to anxiety, again, as we realized our plane was due to leave at 3:30 pm. We were able to purchase a small bunch of bananas for lunch, and around 1:30, a man paddled up to the boat with an envelope, the Captain sounded the horn, and we pushed off right on time.

Thankfully, crossing the great Ganges was uneventful, and we were one of the firsts down the gangplank at 2:30 pm. We had just an hour before the plane took off. Our Samlor driver had the throttle fully open and the squeaky little horn blasting almost constantly as we wove around people, cows, buffalo carts, rickshaws, and occasional vehicles.

It was about 3:10 pm as we approached the south end of the airfield, and I was terrified to see the DC-3 taxing to the north end of the field for takeoff. Again, we began yelling and waving our hands, and as the Samlor reached the building, I jumped out and ran into the lobby, shouting, "stop the plane! We have tickets; please wait."

"Please, sir, have a seat and be calming," an employee answered. "This is the morning flight, which has been delayed. Your flight should return in about 2 hours." We said thank you and goodbye to our friend, the Samlor driver, and his assistant and gave them a nice tip to have dinner together on the way home. We were delighted to enjoy some tea and biscuits while waiting for our flight to Dacca.

At the Dacca airport, we confirmed our flight to Kathmandu, Nepal at 6:20 am the next morning and took the airport shuttle to our hotel. We asked the desk to send our bags up to our room and let the kids bathe as we waited for our bags containing our clothes and toiletries. After 20 minutes, I called inquiring about our bags and was told they'd arrive as soon as the valet returned with the keys. I called again at 7:45. Finally, at 8 pm, we decided to go as we were. Heather wore only a diaper, and Sean and Kerry only had underpants. Carol and I wore dirty travel clothes without the benefit of soap, shampoo, or razor. We looked uncomposed and disheveled in this very fancy and elaborate dining hall, with waiters dressed in tuxedos and tall caps. We allowed the children to play with the piles of silverware until they were served. The service was very prompt, and we soon returned to our room to find our bags miraculously delivered.

Three months later, on November 11, 1970, the Bhola cyclone killed over 500,000 Bengalis and seven months later, in March of 1971, East Pakistan declared independence from West Pakistan, and the war of independence resulted in the new nation of Bangladesh. The change and eerie feelings we experienced, explained.

Our 6:20 am flight on Royal Nepalese Airlines, whose motto might be "We Fly When We Royally Please," made for an exciting day as we finally departed around 3:30 pm in a DC-3, with the front third of the plane loaded with cargo, nets and straps securing it, and us and five other passengers seated on padded benches on the sides. The attendant provided us with cotton balls for our ears and used liberal quantities to seal the cracks around the door. We very much enjoyed our stay at The Shankar Hotel, which appeared to be an old palace.

From Kathmandu, we flew to Patna and then Bagdogra in hopes of riding the little blue train to Darjeeling. We were lucky the clouds allowed us a breathtaking view of Mt. Everest on the flight to Patna but unlucky to find the tracks washed out for the train and had to go by a hair-raising car ride. Our stay in the spacious and elegant "Mt. Everest Oberoi" was memorable.

Back to the lowlands and a flight from Bagdogra to Agra to see the Taj Mahal. The kids wanted to play in the reflection pools but were appeased when we found a courtyard pool that seemed permissible to dangle our feet in before proceeding to the Agra Fort. Then on to New Delhi before catching a flight to Tehran.

In Tehran, we visited with a good friend from East Pakistan working as a Peace Corps administrator and enjoyed visiting with volunteers, shopping, and sightseeing for several days. Carol got a severe headache and did not feel well, so she stayed at Jays' while I took a round trip bus trip up to Chalus on the Caspian Sea. Carol took some antibiotics before we left for Beirut.

We had arranged to meet a classmate from Cal-Poly, Hamid, in Beirut, and he was going to show us his family citrus farm located nearby. Some political activities erupted, and we were not able to get together. Carol felt a little better, so we had a taxi/guide tour of the city and came across several burned and overturned cars, so we went back and walked on the beach.

In Athens, we stayed at a small, homey hotel called Hermanns. We had a balcony overlooking the Acropolis. Carol started feeling bad again and opted to stay at the hotel while I took the kids to see the Acropolis and adjoining ruins. The next day, I took the kids to some other ruins, the National Museum, and a huge market near the harbor while Carol searched for a new antibiotic.

In old Naples, the hotel was old and stately, with lots of darkly polished wood and located near the harbor. After making arrangements to take the hovercraft to the Isle of Capri the next morning, we walked around the old city and enjoyed playing in the parks and the wonderful gelato shops.

A horse-drawn taxi took us to our cabin on the Isle of Capri, and Carol's temperature began to rise again. We made her as comfortable as we could and went down to play on the beach. When we returned, her fever was very high, and she started to become delirious. Asking the resort manager for assistance, he wrote down a doctor's address and agreed to watch out for the kids while I was gone to find him.

The doctor was actually a veterinarian but was able to

help me find ice and wrote down the address of a hospital in Naples. We were on the dock for the first hovercraft the next morning. Carol could hardly walk, and while waiting to board, her eyes rolled back, she wet herself, and passed out. You might imagine my anxiety in getting the kids and bags aboard and going back to grab Carol.

Finding a taxi who could read the directions to the "Napal" hospital took a couple of tries. You cannot know the joy I felt as we entered the gates of the US Naval Hospital. It was difficult to diagnose the cause because of all the antibiotics, but the doctors were fairly certain that it was Dengue Fever or Encephalitis and that she needed to be hospitalized for two weeks with IVs' and close observation.

Given the situation, the doctors agreed that she could be sedated and transported directly home for hospitalization. While she was prepping for release, an aide helped me book flights to Milan, London, and San Francisco. The story of escorting three small children, baggage, and a comatose wife on that final leg was an adventure in itself. We arrived in San Francisco at 10 pm the following evening, and Carol was hospitalized in Memorial North, Modesto for ten days.

We completed the trip home ten years later, on our return from Africa.

Tomorrow we will meet
Death and I
And he shall plunge his sword
Into one who is wide awake
Meanwhile, how grievous the moments
Frittered away.

Dag Hammarskjold, Markings, 1964

APPRECIATION TO:

My mother, Lavena Owens Murry, for saving my letters home. My wife, Linda Chapin Murry, for encouragement and patience. My son, Sean Murry, for technical assistance.

My editor, Ryan Archer, and book designer, Dania Zafar.

Marian Haley Beil, Peace Corps Writers Imprint, for her most generous assistance

Peter Deekle, Community News Editor, National Peace Corps Association.

Made in the USA
Las Vegas, NV
23 September 2024

95698717R00109